HOUSES BY
THE SEA

Emmanuelle Graffin

HOUSES BY THE SEA

With 424 illustrations, 409 in color

 Thames & Hudson

TEMPERATE SEAS

TROPICAL SEAS

Introduction

The Lure of the Sea

People have always been drawn to the coast for a host of different reasons. For some, it has been a means of survival, a place to do business or a gateway to the world. Others have been attracted by its beauty and opportunities for relaxation or recreation. The sea is an abundant resource, and many historic settlements were built close to the shore for easy access to its rich fishing grounds. Towns and cities sprung up around ports across the globe, facilitating the movement of people and goods.

During the 18th and 19th centuries the coast became a fashionable destination. The English upper classes, lured by the perceived health benefits of bathing in the sea, flocked to the coast as a popular alternative to spa towns, and improvements in transport in the Victorian era opened up the emerging seaside resorts to the rest of society. In 19th-century France, it was Empress Eugénie, wife of Napoleon III, and the Duc de Morny, the Emperor's half-brother, who popularized bathing in the sea, particularly along the stretch of coastline between Biarritz, in south-west France, and the Basque country.

Nevertheless, the idea of swimming in the sea for pleasure was long considered ridiculous in the West. Even sailors often could not swim. There are countless stories of ships being caught in a storm, with help arriving too late. The turning point came in the early 20th century, which heralded the dawn of leisure as we know it. Opulent villas were built to meet demand – none more so, perhaps, than those along the French Riviera, which became the playground of the rich and famous.

Building by the Sea

We have been building homes by the sea for a very long time, as evidenced by the discovery of ancient house remains on the Greek islands. The most common materials were stone or wood found in the vicinity. Builders needed expertise and tenacity to combat the effects of prolonged weathering. The heat, humidity and erosion caused by daily exposure to the sun, wind, sand, sea salt and spray are detrimental to man-made constructions. Modern technological advances have led to the widespread use of high-performance materials such as metal, concrete and glass, which ensure greater resistance and comfort.

Coastal topography is no longer an obstacle to construction, whether a building is on uneven land, perched on a cliff, in the centre of a dune field or in the water itself.

An Evolving Habitat

Traditional house design has changed considerably over the centuries. In the past, houses tended to be small and dark, often because building techniques were not sufficiently advanced to construct large spaces, but also to provide protection from the sun or cold. Innovations in the use of concrete, metal and glass allowed for the construction of more spacious residences.

With the advent of the Modern Movement, which aimed to break down the barriers between aesthetics, technology and society, spaces became freer and more fluid, blurring the boundaries between interior and exterior. The development of sophisticated materials such as insulating glass offered greater protection from the elements and allowed architects to take full advantage of views of the sea and the surrounding scenery. In many contemporary designs, the landscape is envisioned as an extension of the interior.

Types of Houses

This book focuses on four types of houses: traditional, natural, unusual and contemporary. The traditional houses are old or are decorated in a way that reflects the local culture. The natural houses are sympathetic to the landscape and climate in design. The unusual houses either jar with the surroundings or do not meet the usual criteria of a home by the sea – a hut or a houseboat, for example. Finally, the contemporary houses represent successful recent collaborations between clients and architects.

Having the opportunity to build an isolated house with direct access to the beach is a rare privilege these days. It also takes a lot of courage, particularly given the climate risk factors that are a feature of modern life. This book contains examples of houses from all over the world, from the Mediterranean coast to the shores of the Atlantic, Pacific and Indian oceans. One of the most striking features of the houses showcased in the following pages is the great care that has gone into securing views of the sea and the natural environment, each seemingly more beautiful than the last.

COOLER SEAS

On the Aran Islands, off the west coast of Ireland, homes are traditionally built using stone and thatch. The low dry-stone walls protect the buildings from the wind all year round.

Cooler seas include the North Atlantic Ocean, the Baltic Sea, the North Sea, the Norwegian Sea, the Barents Sea, the Arctic Ocean and the Antarctic Ocean.

The Atlantic Ocean

The Atlantic separates the Old World of Africa, Europe and Asia from the New World of the Americas. The world's second largest ocean is subdivided along the equator into the North Atlantic and the South Atlantic. Ocean currents in the North Atlantic influence the climate along the east coast of America and Western Europe. The Gulf Stream, for example, channels warm water from the Gulf of Mexico in a north-easterly direction and plays a part in Western

Europe's comparatively clement climate, although the north-east Atlantic is well known for its winter storms, which batter the coasts.

The Baltic and North Seas

The Baltic Sea is comparatively shallow and almost entirely enclosed. Bordered by the coasts of Sweden, Finland, Russia, Estonia, Latvia, Lithuania, Poland, Germany and Denmark, it has weak tides, and its northern subdivisions freeze over in winter. It is connected to the North Sea by a channel that separates Norway and Sweden from Denmark. The North Sea, stretching from the British Isles to Scandinavia, is also relatively shallow, particularly in the southern areas.

The Norwegian and Barents Seas

The Norwegian Sea lies to the north-west of Norway. The numerous fjords that rise from the Norwegian Sea along the coast create a dramatic landscape. Fjords are long, narrow inlets of the sea with steep sides, formed by glacial activity. Filled with salt water, they are often deeper than the adjacent sea. The Barents Sea, framed by Norway, Finland and Russia on the south and Novaya Zemlya on the east, is an outlying portion of the Arctic Ocean.

The Arctic and Antarctic Oceans

Situated at the North Pole, the Arctic Ocean is the smallest of the world's oceans and almost entirely enclosed by Asia, Europe, Greenland and North America. In winter the surface is almost completely frozen. At the South Pole, the Antarctic Ocean or Southern Ocean, the second smallest ocean, links the Indian, Atlantic and Pacific Oceans. It has the strongest ocean current in the world, the Antarctic Circumpolar Current.

Cool Coastal Habitats

Materials such as local stone, brick and wood are a feature of the homes in this section. Doors and windows and the houses themselves are often small in order to protect against the cold winter climate and the violent winds that sweep the coasts. Contemporary houses are also subject to these climate-related constraints.

Drying fish on the Lofoten Islands, off the coast of Norway. The rocks provide this cottage with some protection from the region's violent winds.

Traditional Houses

Many people dream of living by the sea, whether it be in a permanent residence or a temporary hideaway. In some regions, certain factors govern the way that traditional houses are built. Nowadays, architects pull out all the stops to come up with inventive approaches, both in terms of construction and furnishings, to building houses in places that are not naturally suited to human intervention. Every aspect of the project is designed with the specific geographical location in mind,

from environmental concerns to the site orientation and the range of doors, windows and building materials used. From waterfront to half-hidden houses, the possibilities and creative responses are endless. The local climate and environment are often the most important considerations for architects working on traditional coastal homes. Issues relating to heating, resistance to wind and stormy weather, and the complexities of restoring and renovating old houses must be addressed.

A view of the
sumptuous garden at
Maison Quere, Perros-
Guirec, France. Built
on a hillside, the house
overlooks the bay.

Maison Quere, Perros-Guirec, France

This winding garden path, bordered by pink and purple hydrangeas, leads to the house, which looks out over a beautiful beach on the Pink Granite Coast.

Maison Quere is in the small seaside town of Perros-Guirec in the department of Côtes-d'Armor, Brittany. The area is known for the unusual pink granite that characterizes this stretch of coastline. Land and sea are strewn with pink rock formations that have been buffeted into different shapes by the elements.

Built in the 19th century, this traditional house is a typical example of the opulent properties to be found on the Pink Granite Coast. With magnificent views, the house overlooks the bay and is surrounded by an enchanting garden criss-crossed with paths lined with flowers and hedges. Pink and purple hydrangeas, which thrive in the region's slate-rich soil, create an explosion of colour. Like other villas along this coastline, the house features pink granite walls, white-painted shutters and a sloping slate roof.

Bathed in natural light and with extensive views of the garden and sea, the homely living room features a striking cathedral ceiling. The furnishings include comfortable sofas, low fireside chairs and a collection of pottery and bric-a-brac assembled over the years. Many of the objects are inspired by the sea, such as model ships. Items of antique wooden furniture add warmth to the interior.

The room's cottage-style windows are very common in the seaside resorts of the Pink Granite Coast. The largely plain walls are either painted white or decorated with subtly patterned paper. Posters from the 1920s, promoting the local area, hang on the walls.

ABOVE The house is decorated in a simple style, with white walls, family pieces of furniture in light-coloured wood, and a few hints of blue. The owners are keen collectors of pottery and sea-related objects, from model ships to shells.

RIGHT Topped by a decorative panel, the carved door is set in a pointed archway of pink granite. On one side it leads to the first-floor living room. On the other, it opens onto a row of rooms.

White dominates the kitchen, from the floor tiles and walls to the work surfaces. English-style pieces of furniture in light-coloured wood, which have been passed down through the family, add character and warmth. A few hints of blue here and there evoke the sky and the coast. Some of the bedrooms have a wonderful view of the sea and the surrounding countryside. The clean decor matches the classic style of this house perfectly.

Bieke's Hideaway, Nieuwpoort, Belgium

Situated not far from the dunes, Bieke's hideaway stands out with its bright blue shutters. One side of the house opens onto the street, and the other onto the garden.

Nieuwpoort is a small North Sea port on the Yser estuary in a Flemish-speaking region of Belgium. Bieke's hideaway is in the middle of the town, and although close to the beach and the constant bustle of the nearby dyke, it is very quiet. The owner, photographer Bieke Claessens, fell in love with the house as soon as she laid eyes on it, and spent the next two years restoring it. Architect Bart Lens remodelled and renovated the house, retaining the sea views in line with Bieke's wishes.

The cosy, traditional interior contains a mix of designer pieces and bargain or reclaimed items. The cupboard doors in the kitchen, for example, were made from old cheese boards. The exposed beams of the ceiling add height and character to the ground floor, while Bieke has given the TV corner the feel of a beach hut. The new wooden staircase has been varnished to make it look more authentic. The living room has been opened up by replacing brick walls with a partition of poplar panels, and a chimney breast with modern open hearth is the focal point of the space.

OPPOSITE A living room and kitchen were added to the original building. A large picture window opening onto the garden was fitted. Light floods into the room, creating a sense of spaciousness. The period kitchen floor tiles were reclaimed from the original living room.

ABOVE AND RIGHT The new living room is very cosy, with a modern fireplace, comfortable sofas, and a soft, feminine, inviting atmosphere.

In choosing the decor for the house, the owner opted for a largely nautical theme. The white walls, light-coloured, textured concrete flooring, selected items of furniture and use of driftwood help to create a calm, spacious interior.

The first floor contains just two bedrooms, a bathroom, and an additional space which is accessible via a ladder. Plasterboard partitions separate the different spaces, creating a clean, modular look.

BELOW An antique table and a washbasin of Indonesian stone form the washstand.

OPPOSITE A ladder in one of the bedrooms leads to an additional space which can be used as an extra bedroom as required.

Natural Houses

In cooler climes, houses by the sea are not only swept by wind and rain, but are also exposed to extreme temperatures. The natural houses in this section have been designed to offer maximum comfort all year round. The range of decor is striking. In the fisherman's cottage on the Norwegian Lofoten Islands, for example, most of the furniture is second-hand. In contrast, Villa Hector in Knokke-Heist, Belgium, and the stylish house in Torekov, Sweden, are sumptuously furnished.

All the furniture and textiles have been chosen with care, using a colour palette that evokes the sea, sky and land. Built partly using natural materials such as wood, these houses fit perfectly into their surroundings. All of them have a very close bond with the sea, which is reflected in the decor. Despite the often hostile environment, these warm refuges combine comfort and protection from the weather with all the benefits of living by the sea.

The little port of Sakrisøy in the Lofoten archipelago is known for its distinctive wooden cabins, called *rorbu*. The first cabins were built in the 12th century.

Fisherman's Cottage, Lofoten, Norway

Perched on a cliff and sheltered by a large rock, this wooden cottage surrounded by greenery overlooks the bay. As it was renovated on a modest budget, most of the furniture was picked up second-hand at flea markets.

This homely wooden shelter is located on the Lofoten Islands, an archipelago that is part of Norway. Lofoten is a fishing centre situated between Vestfjord – a body of sea which separates the archipelago from the continent – and the Norwegian Sea. In the summer it has twenty-four hours of daylight.

Subject to violent south-westerly winds and other adverse weather conditions, and exposed on a large open area of grassland, the cottage was built against a large rock for protection. Dating from the 18th century, it had been empty for nearly fifty years when the current owners took it over. Artists by profession, they restored the house on a shoestring budget but have successfully created a comfortable refuge from the powerful storms that wreak havoc along the coast.

ABOVE AND LEFT The range of furniture reflects the different types of wood found in this part of the country. Often varnished or painted white or blue, some of this wood comes from the Norwegian boreal forest. The interior decor of this small wooden house is characterized by natural shades on the walls and an eclectic mix of coloured fabrics. The collection of cushions and patchwork bedspreads fits with the well-worn feel of the place.

BELOW The cast-iron wood-burning stove in the kitchen is used both to cook food and to generate heat. Steam from cooking is extracted through a duct. The doors and doorframes are painted in various shades of blue-grey, helping to create a cosy atmosphere.

The cottage comprises a kitchen, a living room and four bedrooms. The owners have tried to preserve its history as much as possible by using local materials such as sand, stone and wood, and by retaining the pictures of fishermen that hung in the bedrooms in lieu of wallpaper. Although wood is an excellent insulator, the cracks between the beams have been filled with foam and fishing nets to prevent heat from escaping. To complement the simple style of the cottage, the owners selected items from their sparsely furnished artists' studio and bought second-hand furniture from local markets. The kitchen and the living room both have old cast-iron stoves, which heat the house during the long cold seasons.

Villa Hector, Knokke-Heist, Belgium

With its red and white bricks and high arched windows, the façade is typical of belle époque architecture in Belgium. The weathervane on the ridge of the slate roof is the height of elegance.

Now a bed and breakfast, Villa Hector is situated at the heart of the Belgian municipality of Knokke-Heist, just a few metres from the sea and the marketplace. Built in 1880, this belle époque villa is typical of the classic urban architecture of the era, with a largely red brick façade and white detailing, high arched windows

and a slate roof. It stands alongside former fishermen's houses and other small residences. When converting the building to a bed and breakfast, the owners were sympathetic to the original design and retained period features such as the painted floor, tiles, and beams which had been hidden behind a false ceiling.

Brick

Bricks are rectangular blocks of fired or sun-dried clay. They have been used as a building material for thousands of years.

> Bricks can be baked or unbaked. Unbaked, they are less resistant to bad weather, particularly rain. Walls are sometimes built using baked and unbaked bricks in alternation, which strengthens the structure. Bricks can also be solid or hollow. Hollow bricks tend to be coated, while solid bricks are often left bare because of their aesthetic qualities. Hollow bricks are very useful due to their thermal inertia and do not require the use of any additional insulation.

> Although brick production was industrialized in the 19th century, bricks were superseded by concrete and steel in the mid-20th century. Nowadays, bricks are often used to clad concrete structures, creating decorative façades.

BELOW The dining room has been decorated entirely in white to make it seem lighter, from the painted wooden shelves and walls to the chairs and tablecloth. Guests are served a traditional English breakfast.

OPPOSITE The kitchen decor is simple yet sophisticated, featuring custom-made oak cupboards with recessed handles, rustic red tiles and white walls and floors.

The ground floor comprises a large living room overlooking the street, a dining room with views of the relandscaped garden which features white roses and lavender, and a kitchen that is accessible via a single corridor.

The six original bedrooms have been knocked through to create three larger, ensuite rooms. Two are on the first floor and one is in the loft space.

The choice of colours reflects the functions of the rooms. While the completely white dining room dazzles guests with its wonderful light, two of the double bedrooms – decorated in more neutral sand and earth shades, in matt finishes – create a calming atmosphere.

All the furniture comes from the Belgian home interiors company Flamant, in order to create a uniform feel throughout the house. In the kitchen, the oak cupboards with recessed handles have been made to measure. Two of the bathrooms with showers are decorated with mosaic tiles, while the third bathroom features a clawfoot bathtub. The bespoke bathroom washstands are made of oak and include recessed washbasins.

The traditional design of the house is inspired by the wealthy, bourgeois lifestyle that characterizes this sophisticated Belgian resort. The luxurious International Style decor is perfectly tailored to meet visitors' expectations.

The first-floor rooms are decorated in shades of sand, grey and natural earth. The filtered light provides a welcome sense of calm after the bustle of Knokke-Heist.

Seafront Style, Torekov, Sweden

Torekov is a small fishing village and summer resort on the west coast of Sweden, by the Kattegat strait. Similar in style to the neighbouring fishermen's homes, this wooden house was built in the 1920s to cater for holidaymakers attracted by the adjoining pebble and sand beaches.

The windows overlook the bay, from which it is possible to see Denmark. The owners have been drawn to the unusual light ever since they inherited this charming abode. They were keen to preserve the history and the memory of the place, while adapting the spaces to their way of life. Thus the old wallpaper has been replaced with white walls, but the traditional pieces of furniture handed down through the generations have been kept.

The house is on two levels. The ground floor comprises a large living room with sea views, a dining room and a kitchen, as well as a workshop belonging to the lady of the house, a textiles designer. On the first floor there are three bedrooms, one of which opens onto a large balcony that takes full advantage of the sea views.

The natural pine floors in all the rooms are original. Blue and grey are dominant colours, echoing the natural environment, and stripes are also a theme of the decor. The owners enjoy watching flocks of sea birds from their living room.

OPPOSITE Most of the walls are hung with seascapes, watercolours and wash drawings depicting scenes from Swedish seafaring history.

ABOVE The old wooden furniture, either varnished or painted primarily in pastel shades, matches the traditional style of the house perfectly.

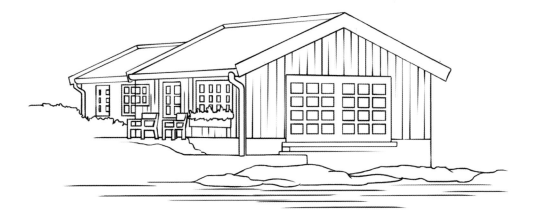

Unusual Houses

The houses described in this section offer maximum comfort in small, non-standard spaces. Built for the most part of wood, a material that naturally lends itself to construction, they all overlook the water – a feature that is reflected in the interior decor, which is characterized by shades of blue and stripes. Although these houses can be lived in all year round, they are perfect for the summer months when they can be thrown open to entertain friends.

The use of space has been optimized to meet everyday needs. It is interesting to see the great lengths that the owners have gone to in decorating their homes exactly to their tastes. A ship's cabin turned bar, versatile wicker furniture, a family accordion to while away the long winter evenings, liner-style deckchairs – these are just a few of the unusual pieces. Faced with the daily onslaught of the elements, these houses demonstrate a flexible approach to living by the sea.

The small island of Smögen is on the west coast of Sweden, surrounded by the waters of the Skagerrak strait. Nestled at the bottom of a small cliff, these fishing huts open straight onto the landing stage.

Bathing Cabins, Nesodden, Norway

ABOVE This is one of
two compact bathing
cabins that function
as additional guest
quarters to a nearby
villa in Nesodden.
Painted white, they
boast stunning views
of the bay of Oslofjord.

Perched on rocks on the Nesodden peninsula in the Oslofjord, in southeast Norway, two bathing cabins belonging to a villa have become summer residences in their own right, marrying comfort with charm. Made of wood, they have been transformed into bedrooms by the young architect Thomas Steen. Original tiles have been preserved in one of the cabins. Intended as additional guest quarters, one of the huts is for parents and the other for children. They have a joint surface area of 10 sq m (110 sq ft), and are only big enough to accommodate beds and wooden washstands. One of the cabins has an outside shower to the rear.

BELOW The cabins are only big enough for beds and washstands. The interiors are decorated in a nautical style, with checked and striped fabrics in shades of blue.

BOTTOM LEFT The iron outdoor furniture and decorative items are sufficiently heavy to withstand the winds, which can be violent in this part of Norway.

BOTTOM RIGHT The cabin washstands are fresh and functional.

ABOVE Made of white-painted wood, the children's hut contains two cabin bunk-style beds. Pastel blue bedspreads coupled with checked and striped cushions complete the look.

TOP LEFT AND RIGHT
Built above the water,
the bathing cabins
have direct access to
the family's boat via a
pontoon.

BELOW Sailing
paraphernalia is stored
in easy-access chests
similar to this one,
which can also be used
as an outdoor tea table
in fine weather. The
wicker furniture is
light and easy to move,
and can be arranged
outside in no time by
guests wishing to make
the most of the sun.

The nautical theme of the interior decor reflects the original purpose of the cabins. They have both been decorated in a similar style, using the same materials and classic seaside colours of blue and white.

Clever storage ideas and a mini-bar refrigerator make the huts highly functional. Easily portable wicker furniture transforms the pontoon into a terrace, from which guests can enjoy a panoramic view of the fjord and the passing boats.

Wooden Chalets, Skagerrak, Norway

These four wooden chalets overlook the Skagerrak strait. The owners like to come here in the summer to make the most of all the sea has to offer.

Surrounded by hills and trees, this property on a small island to the south of Norway comprises four individual wooden houses, the foundations of which are below sea level. The main chalet is devoted to everyday activities. Large sliding doors mark the boundary between the indoor and outdoor spaces. When the weather is bad, visitors can still enjoy a view of the water from behind the glass. The beach hut contains a sauna and a guest room and has a separate entrance. The chalets are equipped with an outdoor shower, enabling occupants to go directly from the sea to the sauna or vice versa. The small guest house is separated from the other chalets by a jetty, adding to the sense of privacy and freedom.

The interior and exterior furnishings have been selected with a great deal of care. The garden furniture and pontoon – home to the sun loungers – are made of teak. Teak is a hard, durable wood with natural water-resistant qualities and is often used on boats. The chalet housing the sauna also contains an outdoor shower.

The interior decor has a nautical theme. The owners like to visit auction houses and antique shops in the summer, and have gradually filled the chalets with model ships, seascapes and other miscellaneous objects. There is even a captain's cabin from an old fishing boat which has been turned into a bar. The curtains and drapes are a harmonious blend of blue stripes and bright colours inspired by nautical flags. The numerous cushions made from flags and pennants are both practical and decorative.

The wooden floors are largely painted, and the walls are for the most part natural wood. The kitchen is an exception: here, the walls are yellow, the work surfaces are teak, and slate tiles cover the floor.

OPPOSITE The walls are covered with an array of maritime art and collectibles, from flags, pennants, seascapes and models to compasses, barometers, pulleys and anchors.

ABOVE This accordion, handed down from the owner's grandfather, still comes in useful during long evenings around the fire.

RIGHT The bright communal areas are both functional and inviting.

Wood

Natural, abundant and long-lasting, wood has been an important construction material for centuries. It is commonly used for post-and-beam framing, roof frames, infilling and cladding.

> Wooden construction is traditional in most areas of northern Europe and North America. Historically, wood can be vulnerable to natural forces such as moisture or fungus, but modern materials and design techniques can limit or prevent damage of this type.

> Wood has many benefits as a construction material. It is relatively cheap, low-maintenance and easy to use as well as providing excellent heat and acoustic insulation. Wooden buildings can provide comfort all year round.

A Floating Home, Hamburg, Germany

This flat-bottomed boat, moored on the Eilbek Canal, is 20 m (66 ft) long and 6 m (20 ft) wide. The owners live and work in this small space, surrounded by the green belt of the canal. The initial idea was to design a houseboat that combined the character of a boat with the comfort of a traditional family home. Designed by the German firm Rost Niderehe Architekten, the boat's key feature is a wall that wraps like a spiral from the outside to the inside and defines the rooms. The daytime rooms (the kitchen and dining room) are on the upper deck – the entrance level – while the private spaces (work, living room, bedrooms and bathroom) are on the lower deck. The living areas are surrounded by a walkway on the lower level and a terrace on the upper level, which protect them from noise and pollution.

Rost Niderehe Architekten

Jörg Niderehe (b. 1975) graduated with a degree in architecture from Georg Simon Ohm University of Applied Sciences in Nuremberg in 2002. Amelie Rost (b. 1981) graduated with a degree in architecture from the same university in 2006. In 2008 they joined forces to set up their own agency. They take existing structures and renovate them according to their clients' wishes and constraints. The construction and renovation projects they work on range from garden sheds to urban construction. They have also converted their own home and workspace, a flat-bottomed boat and a barn respectively.

The architectural language is clear and simple: the wood and metal used are inspired by classic naval architecture. Large picture windows on both levels introduce natural light into the interior. Everything is white apart from the floor, which is natural wood. The decor is simple, with only a few items of furniture in order to maximize space. A 110 sq m (1,200 sq ft) wooden terrace overlooking the canal is a wonderful additional space on sunny days. Houseboating is welcomed in Germany, and the Hamburg regional authorities seem keen to promote this alternative way of life.

The floors are laid with light-coloured wood, the walls and fixtures are white, and the interior is bathed in natural light thanks to large picture windows. Furniture is limited to the bare minimum: beds, sofa, pouffe, dining table and chairs. On a houseboat, the living spaces need to be functional but also designed to withstand any movement on the water caused by the passage of other boats.

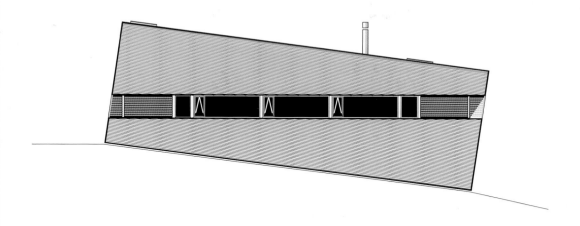

Contemporary Houses

Wood is often used in the construction of coastal homes. It has popular appeal, can be sustainably sourced and offers a high level of comfort. It also ages well, making it an excellent choice for new builds. Wood's natural insulation properties mean lower heating bills in winter and good ventilation in the summer. Architects are forever striving to come up with innovative approaches to using the different varieties of wood available.

In the case of the Sliding House in Nova Scotia, Canada, the quantity of wood used in the interior obviates the need for much furniture: the interior is rich enough, with just a few choice items. The most striking feature of this house, situated on a hill in the middle of an agricultural field, is the roof, which mirrors the slope of the hillside – a bold move by the architect, who designed the house for a family friend. Likewise, El Ray at Dungeness, on the south coast of England, pushes the boundaries of design by adapting a former railway carriage into a kitchen at the centre of the new building. In both examples, the creativity of the architect and the courage of the client are particularly evident.

As its name suggests, the Sliding House looks like it is sliding down the hill. The effect is reinforced by the roof, which follows the slope of the ground.

The Sliding House, Upper Kingsburg, Canada

Built on a hill in the middle of a field, the house benefits from spectacular views of the surrounding countryside. The mix of traditional and modern houses works well here.

The Sliding House is built on a hill on the outskirts of a small agricultural village near Lunenburg, a Unesco world heritage site on the south coast of Nova Scotia, Canada. Built by MacKay-Lyons Sweetapple Architects for a family with three children, the house has views over Romkey Pond and Hirtle's Beach to the east. It is timber-

framed, which is typical of the region, and has a distinctive roof that runs parallel to the slope of the ground. To counterbalance the gradient, the windows on the eastern side run in a horizontal line. The exterior facing is galvanized corrugated iron, while the interior is lined with flush-mounted poplar planks.

MacKay-Lyons Sweetapple Architects

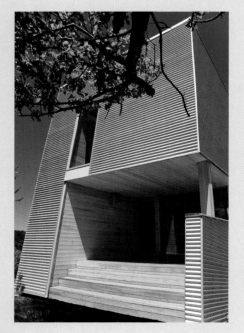

Brian MacKay-Lyons comes from southern Nova Scotia. He graduated with a degree in architecture from the Technical University of Nova Scotia in 1978, and went on to study and work in the USA, China, Japan and Italy. In 1985 he set up his own agency in Halifax before joining forces with Talbot Sweetapple a few years later to form MacKay-Lyons Sweetapple Architects. The agency has gained an international reputation and has won numerous awards for its projects. Brian MacKay-Lyons also teaches at Dalhousie University and is particularly interested in raising awareness of architecture among the general public.

The house has a surface area of around 160 sq m (1,700 sq ft), comprising a living room, dining room, kitchen and bedrooms. The interior design is minimalist, since the wood and the lines of the planks create such a strong statement. The house also features a poplar wood terrace, on which occupants can soak up the sun and the breathtaking views. This highly unusual house is a hybrid between the traditional homes found in this part of Canada and contemporary architecture.

BELOW There are magnificent views of the ever-present coastline from the terrace.

OPPOSITE The interior is finished in richly textured poplar hardwood, rendering any other decoration superfluous. Furniture has been kept to a minimum. Straight lines, minimal curves: it is all about simplicity.

El Ray, Dungeness, UK

This wooden house is situated on Dungeness beach in Kent. A fully glazed south elevation provides views out over the beach and the English Channel.

This timber-clad, curved building, covering approximately 105 sq m (1,130 sq ft), has two bedrooms, a bathroom and a large open-plan living/kitchen area. The house is built around a 19th-century railway carriage, which planners had forbidden from removal. The owners wanted to increase the surface area of the space to accommodate their growing family, while complying with environmental standards.

The new building not only reconfigures the railway carriage as a sculptural centrepiece, but also meets the requirements for protecting the coastline. A sliding glazed wall in the living area affords fantastic views of the bleak, dramatic landscape, which stands in the shadow of the nuclear power station for which Dungeness is known.

Simon Conder Associates

The architect Simon Conder formed his practice in 1984, with offices in London and Suffolk. He also teaches architecture at the Architectural Association School of Architecture and industrial design at the Royal College of Art in London. His practice consists of a small team of architects and designers whose multi-disciplinary expertise is applied to all projects to develop creative, cost-effective solutions within tight time constraints. Their projects are driven by issues of sustainability and energy efficiency, while simultaneously responding to the particular requirements of each client and site.

Enclosed courtyards and the projecting roof over the southern façade offer shelter from the bad weather and winds that batter this coastline. The warm tones of the wood make these spaces inviting.

The house has a symmetrical, bell-shaped plan. The blue railway carriage dominates the main living area at the mouth of the bell and accommodates the kitchen. A large picture window provides an unimpeded view of the English Channel to the south. Smaller windows at the opposite, rounded end of the building provide focused views of the adjacent lighthouse. Two bedrooms and a bathroom occupy this end. Twin courtyards separate the communal space from the bedrooms, and act as suntraps and shelter from the wind. Accessible from inside, the roof offers a 360° panorama of the surrounding landscape, the beach and the sky.

This house scores highly on sustainability and energy efficiency. The well-insulated walls reduce the need for heating and ventilation throughout the year. The house is equipped with a passive solar heating system and a wind turbine for generating electricity. The exterior and terraces are clad in a type of hardwood called itaúba, and the interior is faced in silver birch plywood, both certified by the Forest Stewardship Council. Certification by the FSC ensures that wood and wood products have come from responsibly managed, verified sources. The double-glazed windows are aluminium-framed.

The different colours and textures of the woods used in the interior and the exterior create an interesting effect. The contrast between the warm and cold tones of the interior design and the different building materials is particularly striking.

TEMPERATE SEAS

This large, isolated house overlooking False Bay in South Africa, where the Indian Ocean meets the Atlantic Ocean, takes the traditional lighthouse as its theme. A stone retaining wall supports the wood-clad structure.

This section showcases beautiful houses by the temperate waters of the Mediterranean Sea and the Atlantic Ocean.

The Mediterranean Sea

Semi-enclosed by land, the Mediterranean Sea is connected to the Atlantic Ocean via the Strait of Gibraltar, a narrow stretch of water that separates Europe from Africa. As a result it has limited tides. It stretches some 3,500 km (2,200 miles) in length from Gibraltar to Syria, and is around 790 km (490 miles) wide between France and Algeria. The

Mediterranean Sea has a high salt content and rate of evaporation as well as a complex seabed. Often described as the cradle of civilization, the Mediterranean was a major transport route during antiquity, facilitating commercial and cultural exchange between different peoples.

The Atlantic Ocean

Surface currents in the North Atlantic flow in a clockwise direction. The significant North Equatorial Current is fed by the southwesterly Canary Current, which skirts the north-west tip

of Africa before continuing across the southern stretch of the North Atlantic. In contrast, surface currents in the South Atlantic circulate in an anti-clockwise direction. The cold Benguela Current flows north along the west coast of Africa, while in the west the Brazil Current carries warm water in a southward direction from the Equator. The pattern of currents explains the variations in temperature on the east and west coasts. In contrast to the Mediterranean Sea, this ocean experiences strong tides.

Temperate Living

Traditional houses tend to be made of stone with small windows in order to keep the interior as cool as possible. Contemporary concrete houses often have large windows which maximize the light but also trap heat. Air conditioning is usually installed to combat this, or internal courtyards are incorporated into the design to provide additional ventilation.

The bay at Port-Navalo on the coast of Brittany, France. The marina is enclosed by a breakwater which protects it during the frequent storms. This cedar of Lebanon has fully adapted to the climate.

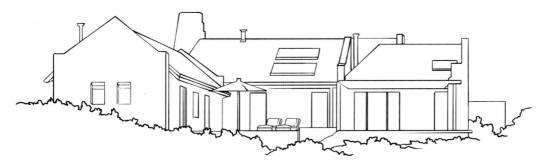

Traditional Houses

Traditional houses by temperate seas range in style from one region of the world to the next. In Europe builders have often used stone. In Greece, for example, where temperatures soar in summer, houses tend to be medium-sized, with small windows and dark interiors to keep the living areas cool; often they are whitewashed on the outside to reflect the sun. In the USA, on the other hand, wood has traditionally been the material of choice, at least until the mid-20th century when concrete took over. These houses met ecological criteria quite unintentionally – a combination of expertise and common sense on the part of the builders – but environmental considerations fell by the wayside with the advent of industrialization. Traditional houses have generally been renovated several times over the centuries, and adapt well to modern comfort requirements.

This house on the Spanish Canary Islands is in a traditional style, with a canal tile roof and whitewashed walls. The unpainted stones add character.

Rocky Shore, Ibiza, Spain

This unusual house, which is made up of three different buildings, is surrounded by greenery. The cobalt blue of the doors and shutters evokes the colours of the Mediterranean Sea.

Nestled in a valley of pine trees, this stone house on the island of Ibiza backs onto an abandoned quarry. The house is made up of three buildings, originally belonging to the quarry, that the owners have spent twenty years renovating. The buildings, which were ruins, have been completely remodelled, with the addition of two bathrooms and a large swimming pool. There are numerous references to the nearby sea throughout the design, from the pebbles in the pathway to the striking cobalt blue doors and shutters.

An enchanting garden encircles the house. Filled with fruit trees, mimosas and flowers, it links the three buildings, creating an exterior space which serves as an additional living area in fine weather.

The outdoor kitchen and living area are sheltered from the sun. White cotton is a prominent feature of this outside space, as well as in the interior.

The uppermost building comprises an outdoor kitchen, dining room and small bedroom. The middle building – the smallest of the three – contains a bedroom and bathroom. As this structure was built onto the face of the cliff, part of the natural rock protrudes into the interior. The living room is located in the third building. A small covered terrace overlooks the swimming pool and provides a magnificent view of the surrounding vegetation. Each room has its own character, and guests are free to choose which one they stay in.

Minimalist and fresh, the decor is perfectly suited to the climate. The bare, unvarnished wooden furniture creates a natural and organic feel.

The white and wooden furniture, shades of pale peach and ochre on the walls and floors, and cobalt blue around the windows and doors all recall Ibiza's colourful past. Power changed hands numerous times, with the island coming under the control of the Phoenicians, Romans and Moors, among others, before finally falling into the hands of the Christians at the time of the Crusades. The furniture and other objects in the house have been picked up over the years from the island's flea markets, which sell a mixture of Mediterranean styles. The owners' lifestyle, the swimming pool, the lush vegetation and the tranquillity of the place exude luxury.

The Naftulin House, Chappaquiddick, USA

Although modern, this wood-clad house was inspired by the New England style. It has wide views of the Atlantic Ocean and the surrounding countryside.

Chappaquiddick Island, off the eastern tip of the larger island of Martha's Vineyard, is in the US state of Massachusetts, on America's east coast. The house is a modern yet low-key holiday home, inspired by the New England style. With wonderful views of the water, the long building clad in cedar shingles comprises two wings linked by a covered passage. Some of the windows are full length, as stipulated by the lady of the house, who wanted to blur the boundary between interior and exterior. A large entrance porch overlooks the untamed countryside surrounding the house and the path to the much-used pontoon.

The interior walls are painted white in order to show off the furniture and other objects – carefully chosen for their rich colours and textures – to full effect.

The owner, an interior designer, chose a limited colour palette in order to showcase her collection of antique furniture, which dates from the 18th, 19th and early 20th centuries. The plain white walls are complemented by the untreated wooden flooring – even in the bathroom – which adds warmth.

The living room contains an eclectic mix of furniture and objects, including a huge sofa, a fireplace flanked by two antique wooden pilasters, a piano used by the owner's daughter, fishing baskets that function as tidies, and a 1970s wooden replica canoe suspended from the high ceiling.

The interior decor is elegant and refined, down to the very last detail. The wooden floors, blinds, furniture and bathroom washstands, as well as the clever use of different textures, add a splash of colour to the white walls and furnishings.

Light floods into the corridor through large picture windows, enveloping the objects on display: two French leather armchairs from the 1930s, an American painting, a portrait from 1910, and an antique jar. The owner likes to adapt furniture to make it more practical: hence castors were added to a butcher's block to adjust its height, while a drawer was fashioned for a 19th-century folding table, transforming it into a desk. An old oak table on the veranda has been painted white to enhance the natural light. This long, graceful house with superb ocean views is the epitome of beautiful design through the successful marriage of old and new.

Villa Bernardi, Santorini, Greece

In the second millennium BC one of the most catastrophic volcanic disasters in history took place – the Minoan eruption – which devastated the island of Thera. Santorini is essentially all that remains of the original island.

Santorini is the largest of a small group of volcanic islands located in the Aegean Sea, about 200 km (120 miles) south-east of the Greek mainland. A popular tourist destination, it is famous for its black sand beaches and for Nea Kameni, an uninhabited volcanic island in the middle of Santorini Bay.

Villa Bernardi is a typical example of the architecture of the Cyclades: small, with narrow windows to protect occupants from the heat and the strong gusts of wind that characterize this region. The whitewashed walls give added protection from the scorching sun in the summer months, and the interspersed pink ochre limestone walls provide a note of originality. The outdoor living area, situated in an alcove, has an unbroken view of the Mediterranean Sea. Villa Bernardi functions as a peaceful sanctuary away from the hustle and bustle of everyday life.

OPPOSITE The whitewashed first-floor terrace carves into the neighbouring buildings. Traditional terracotta jars are arranged decoratively throughout the space. Nowadays they tend to function as planters, although they are sometimes used to store oil and grains as in days gone by.

The small windows restrict light in the interior, helping to protect the house from the searing summer heat. The dark interior spaces are built in such a way that they slot into each other and overlap.

As the floors and bedspreads are white, colour becomes a key decorative element: while some of the doors are natural wood, others are painted orange and green; others still are blue, harking back to the sea and to the superstitions of those who live beside it (blue is said to ward off the evil eye). Some of the doors and windows are round-topped, in the typical style of these houses built into the hillside.

On the first floor, a whitewashed terrace overlooks the bay and is a perfect place for visitors to relax, enjoy the sun and take in some sea air. Like the interior rooms, it is simply furnished, with magnificent, well-patinated terracotta jars, which are arranged decoratively.

Inside, all the rooms are cool and fresh in spite of the outdoor heat, which is often stifling during the summer months.

Natural Houses

The houses in this section have been designed with their natural environment in mind. Like other houses in this book, they have spectacular views and outside spaces in which to enjoy the sun and the sea air, but the surrounding vegetation also plays a key role: from the grapevine on the terrace of a Greek villa on Tinos to luxuriant bougainvilleas at Knysna, South Africa. Sensitivity to nature used to be much more spontaneous than it is today. Nowadays, architects often call on landscape gardeners to help protect, showcase or even re-introduce endemic species of wood, shrubs and vegetation that may be threatened by growing industrialization. The houses in the following section could be viewed as mini conservation areas, where the exterior is as important as the interior.

Like the prow of a boat, the terrace of this villa on the Greek island of Tinos has a stunning view of the surrounding hills and the Aegean Sea in the distance. A bread oven has been built into the stonework.

Vine-Covered Villa, Tinos, Greece

The façade of the central building dates from the 12th century, a period of increasing Venetian control in this part of the Mediterranean. The friezes are made of local slate, which is available in abundance.

This villa dating from the Middle Ages is built on a hillside at the centre of the Greek island of Tinos in the Cyclades. Originally consisting of just one square room, it has been extended over the centuries. The present building was bought in a state of ruin in the 1970s by a young German, who renovated it gradually using local materials – in particular slate, which is available in abundance. Today, it benefits from all the modern conveniences, including air conditioning and a fully equipped kitchen, while successfully retaining its indigenous charm.

BELOW The interior of the house is simple, with plain white walls, in order to highlight the beauty and the character of the building itself. Features include a stone arch, which supports the house, and a bookcase made of slate and stone. The original furniture belonging to the house has been carefully restored according to the owner's specifications.

OPPOSITE A vine arbour over the terrace creates a shady resting place from which to take in the views of the Mediterranean Sea in the distance.

The central room comprises a dining room on one side and a kitchen on the other. Situated on either side of this space, the bedrooms overlook the veranda.

A running theme of the interior design, slate features in several pieces of furniture, from a table and benches to work surfaces, cupboard shelves and a bookcase. The properties of this metamorphic rock make it ideal for cladding, hence its use in the decorative façade of the oldest part of the villa.

The roof has been renovated in the old style: stones rest on a wooden framework and act as tiles. Beneath the roof, a large stone arch dating from the Middle Ages supports the house. The main difficulty in renovating the villa lay in preserving its unique character.

Lagoon House, Knysna, South Africa

Overlooking the Indian Ocean, the garden is filled with bougainvilleas, which add a splash of colour to the stone walls. The house gives the impression of rising up from the rocks on the beach.

This house is situated on the lagoon at Knysna, nestled between the Outeniqua Mountains and the Indian Ocean. Originally a yellow concrete chalet with a waterfront garden, the house has been extended several times over the years by the owners, using local materials.

It features blue shutters and boasts many different living areas – from verandas and patios overlooking the sea to belvederes with views of the garden, where one can breathe in the salty air and listen to the lapping of the waves.

The comfortable interior houses seven bedrooms and a large living room that directly overlooks the sea. The house is furnished with rustic pieces and a collection of objects that evoke the marine landscape. The inspiration for the interior decor comes from the sea, sky and mountains, which are echoed in monochromes of blue, ochre and sienna.

The master bedroom is also painted blue. The large crucifix hanging above the bed in this room was bought from a French antique dealer and is just one example of the great care taken by the owners in decorating the house.

ABOVE LEFT AND OPPOSITE With its veranda overlooking the sea, the house is in complete harmony with the surrounding landscape.

ABOVE RIGHT The owners have collected the various items on display over many years. They are particularly passionate about antiques and like bright colours. The master bedroom is a cheery blue, which seems strangely at odds with the large cross above the bed.

New England Nostalgia, Maine, USA

Maine is the northernmost part of New England, and the easternmost part of the USA. It is famous for its rocky, jagged coasts, low, undulating mountains and immense forests.

This long house on two floors opens onto a large garden with views of the Atlantic Ocean. The house was redesigned by the firm Walter F. Chatham Architect, in response to a client brief to enlarge the existing classic 1950s building.

Inspired by the traditional houses of the region and their simplicity both inside and out, the architect opted for small windows, in stark contrast to the typically open designs of many modern seaside homes. He tried to maintain a balance between windows and walls without sacrificing natural light, and without compromising on the stunning views of the sea and the surrounding countryside.

Walter F. Chatham Architect

Walter F. Chatham was born in the USA in 1952. He studied painting at the New York Studio School and the Philadelphia College of Art before receiving a Bachelor of Architecture from the University of Maryland in 1978. He worked at the Institute for Architecture and Urban Studies, New York, where he was assistant to the internationally renowned architect Peter Eisenman. Chatham founded his present firm, Walter F. Chatham Architect, in New York in 1986. The firm has completed a number of hotel, office and residential projects in New York and Miami, and has received numerous awards. Walter F. Chatham Architect has been associated for the past thirty years with Duany Plater-Zyberk & Company, which founded the New Urbanism movement in the USA. Chatham was an early participant in the environmental design movement.

Assisted by his wife Mary Adams and daughter Sarah Chatham, the architect created an interior that is simple, intimate and warm, in line with the owner's wishes. The oak floorboards, doors and wooden details emphasize the brightness of the white walls. The salt and pepper granite is also a key feature of the interior. It is used for the fireplace surround, the kitchen work surfaces and the flooring in the basement.

In contrast to many buildings in the USA, this house does not have air conditioning but is fitted with large-blade ceiling fans. Clever design features have also been introduced to improve airflow between the different spaces.

An extended version of an existing building, this magnificent country house boasts an impressive layout. The tasteful interior decor is the work of a young designer.

BELOW This lightwell on the first floor, surrounded by a safety railing, improves ventilation between the spaces.

TOP LEFT AND TOP RIGHT Functioning as the main room in the house, the kitchen is built around a central island which serves a dual purpose: not only does it provide a sink and additional work space for the preparation of meals, but it can also be used as a breakfast bar.

ABOVE AND RIGHT When they are not dining, the owners make the most of the leisure space, whether chatting around the fire in the living room, relaxing in the TV room, or settling down with a book on one of the wide, comfortable window seats.

Unusual Houses

Unusual houses tend to stand out along the coastline. Often they leave us wondering who is behind them – an adventurous builder, an architectural historian, a demanding client? Whether they emerge from ruins or a dream, they are remarkable. One of the houses in this section, in a rocky, deserted bay in South Africa, was inspired by a lighthouse. The owners have filled the interior with so many flags and pennants that it feels like a harbour master's office. Another of the houses, on the Spanish island of Majorca, started life as a storeroom and shelter for pigs but was painstakingly restored by the owner over many years in a bid to secure a little corner of paradise by the Mediterranean Sea. Such quirky approaches have resulted in houses that, secretly, we would all love to own.

Brightly coloured huts
on a beach at False Bay,
South Africa.

Clifftop Cabin, Majorca, Spain

Hidden behind pine trees, agapanthus and lavender, this stone house overlooks a creek. A steep stone pathway leads down to the sandy beach.

This house on Majorca, the largest of the Spanish Balearic Islands, clings to a clifftop overlooking the Mediterranean. It was originally used as a storeroom and a shelter for pigs. The owner renovated it gradually, turning it into a secluded haven among the pine trees.

Featuring stone walls and a canal tile roof, the house contains just two rooms: a bedroom and a kitchen. The latter opens onto a large terrace with a magnificent view of the creek below, which is accessible via a stone pathway. The beach is very private due to its limited access.

Stone

Stone has been used as a building material for thousands of years. The ancient Greeks and Egyptians, among others, created monumental stone structures which continue to amaze us to this day.

> Stone can be used as it is or shaped. Stones are usually bound together with mortar or cement, but dry-stone constructions (built without a binding substance) also exist. The main types of rock used in construction include marble, limestone, granite, sandstone, marlstone and slate.

> Over the centuries, stone became the main building material. Around the turn of the 20th century, pioneering steel-frame structures brought metal and glass to the forefront of cutting-edge design in many countries, while concrete became the material of choice after the Second World War.

With terracotta floor tiles and whitewashed walls, the house boasts a simple but elegant interior. The two rooms are separated by an arched doorway which is typical of the region. The bedroom has basic washing facilities, but the shower is outside on the terrace.

The owner wanted to preserve the spirit and history of the building, so he restored the large fireplace in the kitchen and made a feature of the well. Electricity has only recently been installed. The flaky paint of the blue shutters has been left untouched to create a rustic, weathered effect.

With its terracotta tiles, the terrace is the perfect place for sunbathing while listening to the gentle lapping of the waves and the singing cicadas. The outdoor shower is convenient for freshening up.

TOP LEFT The interior comprises a spartanly furnished kitchen and bedroom. An arched doorway connects the two rooms. Shelves built into the wall provide useful storage.

TOP RIGHT A black-and-white curtain keeps the heat out when drawn. The paintings, by a variety of artists, are from a gallery that the owner used to run in the 1980s.

BOTTOM LEFT AND RIGHT The kitchen has a fireplace and a well, which provides water all year round.

BELOW The serene bedroom contains just a few pieces of furniture – a chair, a bedside table, and a bed covered with an indigo bedspread and a mosquito net.

The minimalist furniture from Spain and the Indonesian island of Java has been collected gradually over the years. The interior was envisioned as a restful retreat, and has the peace and serenity of a monastic cell, far from the hustle and bustle of the nearby town.

The terrace, which is protected from the sun by a linen awning, serves as a third room. Covered with the same type of terracotta tile as the interior floor, it comes equipped with an outdoor shower.

Family Retreat, Port-Navalo, France

This large family home overlooks the harbour and the beach. The window frames have been painted blue to evoke the sea.

A former fishing port and pirate haven, Port-Navalo lies in the Gulf of Morbihan, a natural harbour in southern Brittany. This home was built in 1850 and extended in 1990 with a roof conversion, to meet the needs of the owners' expanding family. The façades are natural stone and the roof is slate.

The introduction of lightwells on the third floor and the clever use of shutters increase natural light and the sense of space in the second-floor bedrooms. The picture windows are without glazing bars, so as not to obstruct the magnificent views of the port, the ocean, and a majestic cedar of Lebanon that stands in front of the house.

Despite the focus on the outdoors, the interior is very cosy. The brightly coloured furniture contrasts perfectly with the natural shades of the rest of the house. From the floor coverings to the large sofas, everything seems to have been chosen with rest and relaxation in mind.

Most of the internal walls have been painted white in order to enhance the sense of space and to highlight the exposed stonework of the accent walls, which have been left bare and give the house its authentic character. The decor has a nautical theme, dominated by stripes and shades of blue.

The first-floor living room features a carpet made of sisal – a highly durable material which absorbs ambient humidity – and a 360° fireplace, which fits into the space perfectly. The flooring ranges from terracotta tiles on the ground floor to painted wood in the second-floor bedrooms.

The large terrace at the front of the house overlooking the sea is the perfect place to relax and enjoy the mild microclimate of this area.

BELOW This room is reminiscent of a ship's cabin, with its sliding door, wooden and white canvas steamer chair, commode chest and clever use of space.

OPPOSITE This bedroom has been furnished simply, with just the natural stonework of the wall and the blue-painted beams and ornamental band below the dado rail for decoration.

In the main bedroom, the wooden ceiling beams have been painted blue and a decorative band has been added below the dado rail, in stark contrast to the other rooms which are typically white. These splashes of colour work well with the exposed stone wall. Much like a ship cabin, every nook has been put to use: a desk slots neatly into a third-floor dormer, for example. The furniture and decorative items have been carefully chosen. The lamp, commode chest and chairs pictured here are items we might associate with life at sea. Even the bathroom walls are decorated with blue mosaic tiles.

Lighthouse, False Bay, South Africa

This lighthouse-inspired home overlooks False Bay, a body of water defined by Cape Hangklip and the Cape Peninsula in south-west South Africa. Positioned between the Indian and Atlantic oceans, it has a unique atmosphere: the quality of light, surrounding rocks and uninterrupted views of nature together give the impression that the house stands at the edge of the world. Indeed, it was the location that inspired the outward appearance of this square, wood-clad structure. A tower resembling a lighthouse rises up out of the corrugated iron roof and is totally in keeping with the remote, coastal location of the house.

OPPOSITE The strong nautical theme throughout the interior spaces – including seascapes, model ships, chests, shells, and furniture made of natural materials such as wood and wicker – adds character to the otherwise plain decor.

The interior layout is simple, consisting of an open-plan kitchen, living and dining area on the ground floor, and three bedrooms and a workshop on the first floor. The central tower houses a staircase with a railing sculpted to resemble the contours of a lighthouse. The windows at the top of the tower are decorated with a variety of colourful flags, which are also visible from the outside. The Union Jack adds a splash of colour to the monochrome spaces of the ground floor, with its bold blue and red, geometric lines. Model ships, chests and wicker furniture are recurring elements of the interior design, creating a warm, harmonious atmosphere.

ABOVE The Union Jack flag is another prominent feature of the design, whether it is draped over a table, on a cushion cover or in one of the windows in the tower. For the British owners, it not only adds a touch of colour but reminds them of their roots.

This all-season house successfully blends traditional and modern styles, from the brick fireplace and wrought-iron bed to the wooden and wicker pieces. The nautical items work well with the modern furnishings such as the designer Italian lamps.

On the first floor, the white walls and exposed ceiling beams reflect the abundant natural light, making even the smallest rooms of the house feel bright and airy. Marine navigation lights have been fitted to the walls just below the ceiling, continuing the nautical theme.

The owners have carefully combined different materials, textures and motifs to great effect, giving the house a warm and feminine feel.

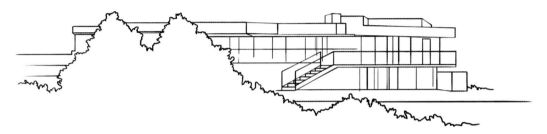

Contemporary Houses

Nowadays, architects are faced with the challenge of designing and building houses that both meet their clients' requirements and satisfy the strict standards which have been set for environmental protection. The various factors at play can sometimes lead to surprising projects that offer innovative solutions to wider construction and housing-related issues. The architect or designer may experiment with different building materials or approaches to interior design, pushing the envelope to create a house that marries modernist style with contemporary sensitivities. The houses in this section are among the finest examples, using advanced construction materials such as concrete, wood shingles and glass to produce design-led, functional, sustainable structures.

A glass façade at Villa Sacha, Cannes, France, reflects the stunning sea views.

Villa Sacha, Cannes, France

Clean lines define the
elegant Villa Sacha,
which fits in perfectly
with the surrounding
countryside.

Built on a hillside overlooking the bay of Cannes on the French Riviera, Villa Sacha is characterized by clean, horizontal lines and a spectacular cantilever roof so that it seems almost to float between the sky and the sea. Originally built in the 1970s, it has been completely refurbished; the interior load-bearing walls were demolished and replaced with concrete beams. The lush garden, which contains mimosas, santolinas, agaves, yuccas and euphorbias, among other plants, was designed to showcase the ultra-modern structure. The deck of the infinity pool is laid with Bateig tiles, while black vitrified tiles line the pool itself, making the water appear darker than the sea and the Lérins Islands in the distance.

Glass

Glass is a hard, fragile, breakable and transparent material. It is produced by fusing silica, the main constituent of sand, with basic oxides.

> Although glass has been used in windows for hundreds of years, it was only in the 19th century, with advancements in manufacturing processes, that its true potential began to be realized. During the 20th century it became an integral element of architectural design, from the International Style buildings that emerged in Europe and the USA in the 1920s and 1930s to modern skyscrapers.

> This versatile material has proven that it can meet modern requirements for safety and design, and that it can be used innovatively to achieve energy efficiency and sustainable development. The qualities of glass can be varied to manage solar gain and heat loss to suit climate conditions.

Villa Sacha has two wings. The spacious living quarters, where occupants can while away the day, are at garden level. The sleeping quarters, comprising eight bedrooms and the bathrooms, are on the upper level. The choice of materials is perfect for the simple, elegant lines of the interior: concrete, glass and Bateig tiles for the interior and exterior floors, along with various different types of wood veneer for the interior. The living areas, which are based on the principles of light and shade and the interplay of transparency and opacity, all open onto large outdoor terraces.

BELOW The large picture windows in the Corian kitchen offer spectacular sea views. Sheltered from the wind, the main courtyard behind the kitchen is paved with black gravel.

OPPOSITE From the living room to the bathroom, every space in the house has been designed to maximize the views.

BELOW The washbasins and mirrors are by the Italian company Boffi.

OPPOSITE The Corian bathtub in one of the bathrooms has wonderful views of the bay of Cannes.

The tasteful furniture is by a variety of famous contemporary designers. Some items have been made to measure, notably the low, stained oak tables in the living room. White Corian has been used in the kitchen and bathrooms. Some of the interior walls have been painted anthracite grey, which contrasts with the white pieces and dark wood.

The walk-in wet area pictured below, separated from the rest of the room by a discreet glass panel, is yet another example of the designer playing with transparency.

Eastern Tranquillity, Bodrum, Turkey

Nestled into a hillside, the villa overlooks the sea and the surrounding countryside. The swimming pool fits in perfectly with the natural environment and is ideal for cooling down in the summer.

The port town of Bodrum, in south-west Turkey, is very popular with visitors from Istanbul and tourists. This villa, which belongs to a wealthy antique collector, is hidden in the hills scattered with cypress and olive trees that surround the ancient town. Vedat, the owner, wanted a high-tech version of a traditional Turkish house, and chose the well-known design duo Gökhan Avcioglu and Hakan Ezer for the task. The villa, built from local stone, is sympathetically designed to blend into the surrounding landscape. From the deceptively spacious living areas, the wrap-around balcony and the outdoor swimming pool, there are stunning views of the sea.

BELOW A closed-hearth
fireplace separates the
living room from the
dining area. The antique
items on display set off
the modern furniture to
great effect.

OPPOSITE The low-rise
villa virtually disappears
into the surrounding
countryside.

All the rooms in the villa are arranged around an open, central room, a typical feature of Turkish homes. The living room and dining room are on the ground floor. The fully glazed south elevation introduces plenty of natural light into these spaces.

The walls are made of prefabricated perforated concrete slabs, and the concrete floor was cast in situ. The bespoke, state-of-the-art kitchen features an epoxy resin floor, Corian work surfaces and oak cupboards.

The bedrooms and bathrooms are on the first floor, which is more traditional in style. The low ceiling of the upper level makes it feel more intimate.

The owner's passion for antiques is subtly conveyed through the eclectic mix of items on display, which include a charming oval portrait of a woman. On the first floor, these treasured items blend perfectly with the architecture of the house. Each decorative piece has its own place on the villa's various shelves and bookcases.

The owner wanted an ultra-functional kitchen: oak, Corian and epoxy resin increase the modern feel of this space.

The interior design effectively combines modern and traditional elements. The concrete floors and walls contrast with the antique furniture and objects on display, which include a Chinese Ming-period opium bed, a hollow Anatolian tree trunk, 18th-century English chairs, Roman glassware and dervish hats. In the dining room, marble columns used as table legs stand alongside a 17th-century Dutch sideboard and a marble chandelier. On the first floor, traditional costumes are used as lampshades, and colourful kilims cover the floor.

Waterfront Estate, Long Island, USA

Overlooking Oyster Bay, this large house has wide views of the surrounding countryside, but retains a sense of privacy thanks to the use of concrete arches.

This large, contemporary home is situated on Long Island in the state of New York, and overlooks Oyster Bay and Connecticut. Built for a couple and their five children, it can accommodate both family and friends. The owners wanted a house which was interesting both outside and inside, but which was also sheltered in order to preserve their privacy. They also

wanted to be able to enjoy views of their garden and the bay at any time.

The firm of architects commissioned to build the house, Grandberg & Associates, therefore designed a house within a house: walkways, garden views and some living areas have been incorporated into the outer structure; the private living spaces are located in the inner core, however.

Grandberg & Associates Architects

Ira Grandberg graduated with honours from Columbia University School of Architecture, New York. He set up his agency, Grandberg & Associates, in New York in 1976, and gradually built up a staff of multi-disciplinary and experienced architects. Grandberg oversees each project and dedicates himself to providing each client with a high level of personal attention and commitment throughout the design and documentation process. The firm specializes in private residences and estates, historic restoration, corporate interiors and retail, and is mainly active in the USA.

BELOW In the manner of a country house, this large residence can accommodate the entire family and any guests.

OPPOSITE Next to the window in the first-floor study is an LC4 Chaise Longue, designed by Le Corbusier, Charlotte Perriand and Pierre Jeanneret.

The building is made of white-painted concrete. The lower floor comprises the guest quarters and the children's rooms. The upper floor, which has a simple circulation pattern, is reserved for the parents. A shared walkway separates the two floors visually and acts as a soundproofing barrier. Large external windows frame views of the surrounding countryside, the sea and the sunsets, and allow the owners to enjoy the changing of the seasons.

All the floors are covered in the same stone, in order to unify the space. The interior decor is simple but luxurious, featuring, among other things, early 20th-century furniture designed by Le Corbusier.

TROPICAL SEAS

The tropical seas section includes the Pacific Ocean, the Indian Ocean and the Caribbean Sea, also known as the Sea of the Antilles.

The Pacific Ocean

The Pacific is the world's largest ocean, covering around one third of the earth's total surface. Surrounded by Asia, Australia and the Americas, and bounded in the south by the Antarctic Ocean, it includes Asian islands and archipelagos such as Japan and the Malay Archipelago as well as Oceania. The Pacific contains the deepest trenches in the world, some exceeding 10,000 m (33,000 ft), and experiences frequent earth tremors. It also contains many coral reefs. Pacific currents generally flow in a clockwise direction in the Northern Hemisphere, and anti-clockwise in the Southern Hemisphere. The North Equatorial Current is one of the most significant, following a path from east to west. The warm Kuroshio Current flows in a northerly direction and forms the western boundary of the North Pacific.

The Indian Ocean

The Indian Ocean is the third largest ocean on the planet, covering some 75,000,000 sq km (29,000,000 sq miles). It is bounded to the north by India, Pakistan and Iran; to the east by

Burma, Malaysia, Indonesia and Australia; to
the south by the Antarctic Ocean; and to the
west by Africa and the Arabian Peninsula. The
southern part of the Indian Ocean features an
anti-clockwise system of currents which drives
the South Equatorial Current.

The Caribbean Sea

The Caribbean Sea is situated to the east of
Central America and south-east of the Gulf
of Mexico, in the Atlantic Ocean. Covering
an area of approximately 1,940,000 sq km
(750,000 sq miles), it is at its narrowest along
the Windward Islands, at its easternmost
boundary, and at its widest between Panama

and Cuba. The Caribbean has been a busy
route of travel and transport for several hundred
years, but the opening of the Panama canal in
the early 20th century transformed it into one
of the great ship highways of the world.

Sun, Sea and Sand

A wide variety of materials have been used
to build the houses in this section, including
stone, wood and concrete. The windows
tend to be large to take full advantage of the
beautiful sea views and warm weather. The
architecture often contains numerous local
references, and in countries such as Mexico
the walls are commonly painted in earth tones.

The sumptuous,
beautifully maintained
garden of Morabito
Art Villa, Bali, has
wonderful views out
over the ocean. It
contains lily ponds and
a swimming pool.

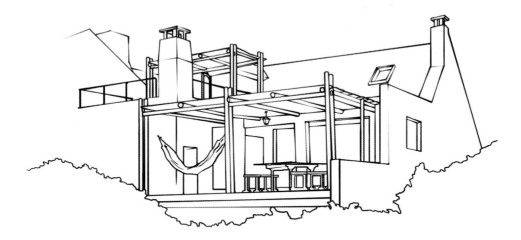

Traditional Houses

Part of the charm of older-style houses lies in their connection to the past. Both houses in this section give the impression of being perhaps older than they really are. The wood-clad cottage in Hawaii, with its slate tiles and white-painted door and window frames, is reminiscent of historic houses on Nantucket Island, Massachusetts. The cosy interior is equally traditional in style, furnished with local second-hand pieces and other objects. Although the 1970s-style holiday home in Malibu, designed by Brian Tichenor, may look more contemporary than the Hawaiian cottage, it too has traditional elements. These houses benefit from modern comforts, including sumptuous pools, but fit in perfectly with the surrounding coastal landscape as if they had always been there.

Diverse in style, these houses on the Malibu coast overlook the Pacific Ocean.

Cottage in Hawaii, USA

On one side, this cottage boasts views of the Pacific Ocean and the beach dotted with agave plants; on the other, it overlooks the well-maintained garden and newly built swimming pool. Tradition and modernity have been successfully combined here to create a warm, inviting family home.

This cottage on the island of Hawaii overlooks the Pacific Ocean. The owner and her husband were looking for a seaside holiday home for themselves and their three small children when, quite by chance, they came across this house. With its wood cladding, slate tiles and white-painted door and window frames, the cottage

is reminiscent of the traditional style of housing on historic Nantucket Island, Massachusetts. They fell in love with it, and went on to completely renovate the interior, build a swimming pool and convert the utility rooms next to the garage into guest quarters. A large balcony on the first floor has great views of the beach.

BOYS

Colour is used to define the spaces: red and brown in the master bedroom, mint green staircase treads, pale yellow in one of the bathrooms, and turquoise in the other.

The owners have furnished the interior with antique furniture from local dealers. Most of the walls are plain white, but a range of colours are effectively used to define the various spaces, including grey green, mint green, turquoise, light blue, beige, red and burgundy. The parquet floors are repainted every year as a kind of ritual.

A distinctive Hawaiian influence characterizes the interior decor, from the all-white guest room, which features bunk beds and a wardrobe decorated with painted shells (pictured below, bottom right), to the bathroom display of starfish, sponges, razor shells and beach pebbles (top centre).

LEFT One of the guest rooms overlooking the sea has been painted completely white, including the furniture, in tribute to the wise men and women of the island who would spend entire days in prayer.

Only the shells inlaid into the wardrobe evoke the sea and act as a reminder that the island, usually so peaceful, can at times become the plaything of the elements, struck by storms and hurricanes.

Seventies Spirit, Malibu, USA

The garden is dominated by different species of grasses.

The owners of this house wanted a home they could escape to during the holidays, when Los Angeles became too much. The couple called on architect Brian Tichenor and interior designer Madeline Stuart to turn their dreams into reality. The brief was ambitious: to build a house that was comfortable and cosy as well as modern and minimalist. The result is a symphony of earth tones. All the downstairs rooms open onto a large garden full of grasses and trees. A large wooden deck overlooking the Pacific Ocean features a swimming pool.

BELOW The house is light and airy, with large windows and balconies.

OPPOSITE Paintings by American artist Richard Serra flank the imposing site-cast concrete fireplace in the living room. Serra is best known as a minimalist sculptor.

The interior decor is vintage 1970s in style. The furniture includes pieces by well-known designers and was bought primarily from antique dealers and specialist boutiques. The richly textured, hand-finished walls are reminiscent of windswept sand and Zen gardens. The colour scheme was chosen to evoke the sea and the sunsets: for example, the tiles in different shades of blue in the kitchen, and the touches of orange in the lounge and one of the bedrooms. The house is dominated by natural shades that echo the external environment, in line with the owners' wishes.

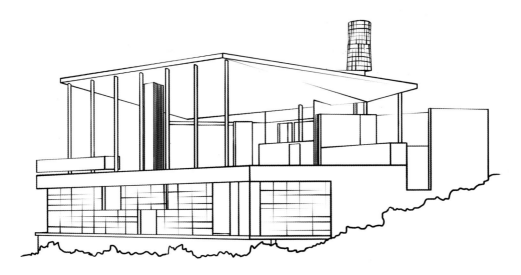

Natural Houses

These houses have an almost seamless connection with nature and local culture. Particular care has gone into the design of the gardens. The Morabito Art Villa, Bali, integrates a collection of Indonesian art with a luxuriant tropical landscape. Casa Fantastica in Mexico, perched high above the sea, enjoys stunning views and wonderfully rich colours, from blue expanses to lush greens to the striking red of the house itself. Paraty House in Brazil, on the other hand, takes full advantage of its cantilever design to introduce green spaces overlooking the bay. All three are modern but have used local materials and building techniques, especially Casa Fantastica with its red ochre walls and thatched roof.

Casa Fantastica's red ochre walls and painted woodwork are typical of Mexican architecture.

Casa Fantastica, Puerto Vallarta, Mexico

The villa is characterized by the volumetric interplay of the different spaces and by the rich textures of the materials used, including the thick red ochre walls, thatch, glass and wood.

This sumptuous villa, perched on a hillside overlooking the Pacific Ocean, lies between the popular Mexican resort of Puerto Vallarta and the city of Manzanillo. Surrounded by dense jungle, it dominates the surrounding area with its thick red ochre walls and thatched roof, which are designed to offer protection from the sun.

The doors and windows are large to allow the refreshing sea breeze to pass through the house both day and night. Vine-wound palm trunks make attractive columns. The concrete floor is decorated with arabesques of black pebbles. A large terrace looks out over the bay.

Whether reclining on
one of the terraces or
lying in a hammock,
this is the perfect place
to relax. Everything in
the house is geared to
the hot climate, from
the steamer chairs by
the swimming pool
to the hammocks and
patios in the shade.

Thatch

Thatch is straw, reeds or similar plant material that is used as a roof covering. In Europe it has been used for this purpose for many centuries. In much of the UK, thatch was the principal roofing material until the Victorian era, when it was abandoned in favour of tiles and slate.

> Thatch is experiencing a resurgence in popularity thanks to its heat and sound insulation properties. Modern thatched roofs are more compact thanks to advances in tools and the use of fireproofing materials.

> Thatched roofs are expensive to make because they require specialist expertise. A thatched roof is 30 cm (12 in.) thick on average and needs a pitch of 45° to ensure the run-off of precipitation. The framework of the building must also be strong enough to take the weight of the thatch as well as snow or any sand, dust or moss which may accumulate over the years.

Colour is everywhere: the swimming pool, walls, fabrics and natural wood are all rich in nuances. The use of lively, dynamic colours reflects the owners' personalities.

The furniture is rustic in style, from benches and beds cut from solid stone and dressed with magnificent fabrics to items made from tropical wood which resemble functional sculptures. The house has six bedrooms, all offering wonderful views of the ocean.

The sky-blue infinity pool overlooks the surrounding tropical vegetation – perhaps most notably the striking cacti – and the beach. The steamer chairs offer the perfect platform from which to admire the bay. A refreshing water feature in black polished concrete decorates one of the patios. The end result – a building that is both modern and timeless – is a celebration of traditional Mexican architecture.

Morabito Art Villa, Bali, Indonesia

The indigenous art exhibited in the grounds perfectly complements the luxuriant vegetation of the tropical garden, transforming it into an oasis of relaxation and calm.

Built and furnished by the French architect and jewelry designer Pascal Morabito, this villa on the west coast of Bali overlooks the bay of Kuta and Jimbaran. Combining contemporary style and traditional heritage, it is set in the heart of a one-hectare (2.5 acres) park dotted with palm, coconut and frangipani trees – a green expanse that fronts the Indian Ocean for some 150 m (500 ft).

With its private garden and panoramic views of the sea, the villa is a veritable haven of peace. It is home to a vast collection of contemporary and indigenous Indonesian art, which is displayed around the park and inside the various buildings.

Pascal Morabito

Pascal Morabito is extremely versatile. He studied architecture but is active in a wide range of fields, including jewelry design, china, crystal and glassware, fine watches, perfumes, cosmetics, leather goods, fashion, accessories, interior design, home furnishings, sculpture, architecture, photography, well-being and lifestyle. The indigenous art collection on display at the Balinese villa reflects his passion for archaeology. Just as an archaeologist casts light on the lives of our forebears, Morabito opens a dialogue with the past by presenting ancient artefacts in a highly contemporary setting.

BELOW Views of the seafront (top) and the Canopy suite (bottom), which has two private swimming pools.

OPPOSITE Inspired by traditional architecture, the Majapahit suite is a house with a private garden, decorated in a typically Indonesian style. Lush vegetation surrounds the modern and traditional architecture to create a harmonious whole.

The main house has a living area – the so-called 'Bale' – comprising a large reception room, dining room with wood-burning stove, kitchen, bar, home cinema, library, and a large terrace which opens onto the garden, the swimming pool and the sea. The Bolare suite, which is on the first floor, looks out over the sea. The Canopy suite is situated above the large living area. The Majapahit suite is a house with a private garden. Guest quarters are housed under a thatched roof, a rare feature in modern architecture. Finally, nestled among the trees is a spa with sea views.

The park boasts antique sculptures, a spa and a children's tree house. One of the suites has a large outdoor bathtub (opposite below), a hollowed-out rock from the island of Java. The wooden floor is in keeping with the natural surroundings.

From materials such as wood, stone, bronze and thatch to the warm decor and natural light, everything has been designed with nature – the architect's source of inspiration – in mind. The impeccably manicured tropical garden wraps around the various buildings and sets off the blend of modern and traditional design. The exterior spaces include seating areas, tree houses, pathways and ponds as well as a unique 'tree spa': water cascades from a tree trunk into a hollowed-out rock and transforms it into a relaxing bath.

The stone constructions and sculptures, swept by the sea breezes and salty air, seem to melt into their environment. Every aspect of the design suggests luxury, peace and pleasure.

Paraty House, Brazil

The house makes use of an attractive variety of materials and textures: concrete, glass, stone and eucalyptus panels.

This house is situated in Paraty, an old colonial town between Rio de Janeiro and São Paulo. Surrounded by rain forest, it consists of two reinforced concrete boxes, one on top of the other, in a design inspired by the pioneering architects Le Corbusier and Frank Lloyd Wright.

Designed and built by the Brazilian architect Marcio Kogan, this house projects out from the mountainside in an 8 m (26 ft) cantilever. Huge glass windows line its

27 m (89 ft) span and look out over the Atlantic Ocean. Residents arrive at the house by boat, and access the building via a bridge which leads to a stone staircase beneath the lower box.

The roofs of both boxes have been transformed into terraces, and are used by the owners as observation decks from which to admire the sea, sky and surrounding vegetation. The terraces contain sculptures, plants and herbs.

Marcio Kogan / Studio MK27

Studio MK27 was set up in the early 1980s by Marcio Kogan, who graduated from Mackenzie University, São Paulo, in 1976. The agency employs a number of architects and collaborates with professionals around the world to create designs of formal simplicity. Overseeing projects from beginning to end, they place considerable importance on achieving harmony between architecture and nature. Great care is taken over details and finishes, with concrete, dry stone and wood among the materials of choice. Studio MK27 has won several awards including the Record Houses, the D&AD 'Yellow Pencil' and the Dedalo Minosse.

BELOW The terrace gardens overlook the sea.

OPPOSITE The interplay of light and space is an important element of the design, used to great effect in the planted interior courtyard, glass partitions, and retractile panels of eucalyptus in the bedrooms. The designer furniture is in complete harmony with the ultra-contemporary architecture, which in turn fits in perfectly with the surrounding natural landscape.

The house has a total surface area of 1,000 sq m (11,000 sq ft), which includes a living room and kitchen on the lower floor and bedrooms on the upper. Designed by Suzana Glogowski, the meticulously finished interior is an ode to simple lines and is shown off to maximum effect by indirect lighting. It is furnished with sculptures, murals by famous artists, and a fine selection of contemporary furniture.

The design of the house allows sunlight to flood into the interior spaces. The areas facing the mountain have small interior patios that diffuse the penetrating rays and illuminate the exposed reinforced concrete partitions, giving them a striking texture. In the bedrooms, retractile panels of eucalyptus protect the interior from the sun while allowing the trade winds to enter.

The roof terraces add another dimension to the house, with their walkways, plants and views of the sea and surrounding countryside. The large wooden terrace overlooking the pool is the perfect place to relax.

The vastness of the interior space only serves to enhance the impression of luxury created by the exterior of the house and its garden.

Unusual Houses

These houses seem out of place in their surroundings and yet integrate perfectly, as if they had always been there. Rising up out of the sand in Mozambique, the Aranda da Silva House in Ponta do Ouro reflects modern architectural vocabulary with its white-painted concrete, dark wood and large picture windows. At the same time, its corrugated iron roof jars with the environment and suggests a precarious habitat that could fly away at the slightest gust of wind. The house at Las Arenas in Peru, a compact parallelepiped in the middle of the beach with barely any garden to speak of, could be mistaken for a UFO that has fallen from the sky. Everything is contained in the house, which appears suspended above the lawn: even the swimming pool is part of the structure.

The beach house at Las Arenas, Peru, appears suspended above the lawn, creating a sense of weightlessness .

Beach House, Las Arenas, Peru

Designed by the Peruvian architect Javier Artadi, this beach house is situated around 100 km (60 miles) south of Lima. With the ocean on one side and the Atacama Desert on the other, the house cleverly plays on its location between these two different habitats, where land meets sea. The concrete structure, which resembles a white box with clean, straight lines, projects from a dark grey base as if suspended above the lawn. At the front of the house, there is a small swimming pool and a patio that serves as a dining room and open-air living room, and looks directly out over the beach, the Pacific Ocean and the distant horizon.

Javier Artadi / Artadi Arquitectos

Javier Artadi graduated from the Faculty of Architecture and Urbanism at Ricardo Palma University in Lima, Peru, in 1985. He set up his agency in 1986, and has since completed numerous projects in fields such as urban planning, public infrastructure, civic and cultural buildings, offices and workplaces, private houses and product design. He has won numerous international competitions and received many awards and distinctions. In 2000 he became a professor of architecture at Universidad Peruana de Ciencias Aplicadas (UPC). He was a finalist in the IV Latin American Biennial of Architecture with the beach house project in Las Arenas. He has been invited to present and display his work in South America, Europe and the USA.

The house was designed for a couple and their three children. With a surface area of just over 200 sq m (2,300 sq ft), it comprises four bedrooms, a kitchen, a dining room, a bathroom and a utility room. A long diagonal corridor, which divides the rooms, recalls the house's location at the boundary between land and sea. The living spaces are separated by large glass sliding doors, through which the beach is always visible.

The surrounding views are framed by apertures and cutouts in the structure, which trace a succession of solid and empty spaces that control the movement of light and air. The minimalist decor is in perfect harmony with the architecture. Modest in size, the garden is a simple, bare lawn.

External spaces form part of the overall structure of the house, which is furnished in a minimalist style.

The Aranda da Silva House, Ponta do Ouro, Mozambique

Located in south-east Africa, Mozambique boasts a long stretch of coastline on the Indian Ocean. This former Portuguese colony is the second-largest Portuguese-speaking country in the world by population and the third-largest in terms of surface area.

This waterfront house in Ponta do Ouro, in southern Mozambique, is just a few kilometres from the South African border. Overlooking the dunes, it has been built on a site that is surrounded by greenery and preserves the natural shape of the land. The building sits fairly low to the ground, which shelters it from the hurricanes that are common in this part of Africa.

The house is characterized by light and transparency throughout the various spaces. The timber framework on a solid masonry base allows for large windows without weakening the structure.

José Forjaz Arquitectos

José Forjaz was born in Portugal in 1936. He graduated from the Academy of Fine Arts in Porto with a degree in architecture in 1966, and then completed a masters in architecture at Columbia University, New York, in 1968. He set up his agency in Maputo in Mozambique in 2001, and now heads up a small team. José Forjaz Arquitectos undertakes all kinds of architecture-related projects, from urban planning and design to private residences, apartment blocks and buildings for institutional, religious and educational purposes. Forjaz works across Africa, and in Mozambique in particular. He is a proponent of social justice and sustainable development.

BELOW White fabrics and dark wood characterize this small living room, complementing the plain walls and exposed timber framework.

OPPOSITE White also dominates the patio area, from the walls to the floor tiles.

Modest in size, the house has two living rooms, a dining room and three bedrooms. With stunning views of the Indian Ocean, it is a great place to watch the sun go down. The contrast between the dazzling white structure and the dark wooden framework is striking.

A long metallic roof covers the house like a canopy, shading the external seating areas. A large trellis erected over the patio is designed as an extension of the interior, with climbing plants creating a natural roof.

BELOW When the sun begins to set, it is time to enjoy the spectacular views from the terrace before sitting down to supper.

OPPOSITE The large table at the heart of the fitted kitchen ensures that every mealtime is a special occasion.

The building is accessed via a short flight of steps leading to a living room, which is decorated simply with plain white tiles and furnished with black and white upholstered pieces that echo the colours of the building. Wicker seating on the terrace, which boasts fantastic views, creates an additional space for relaxation. With its minimalist simplicity and natural setting, the house is an oasis of calm for the city-dwelling owners, who use it as a holiday home.

Caribbean Colours, St Barts, French West Indies

The house offers a magnificent view over this amazing Caribbean bay. An open-air lounge area makes the most of the garden and sea views, with a white canvas canopy to provide shade.

This spacious and striking house is set on the rocky island of St Barts in the Caribbean. Built from concrete by the agency In Store, it opens onto a garden filled with luxuriant tropical plantlife. A swimming pool looks out over the bay.

The outdoor lounge area is shaded by a white canvas canopy and equipped with couch seating that echoes the turquoise blue of the pool. White recliners on the wooden decking allow sun-worshippers to relax and enjoy the scenery.

The clean, modern architecture is predominantly white, but subtly punctuated with touches of colour: a bright pink wall, a red lacquer coffee table, a black floor. The house seems perfectly integrated with the lush vegetation outside.

With its window blinds that recall colonial buildings in the region, the house offers an intriguing interplay of spaces and volumes, with several wooden staircases allowing direct access to the outdoor terraces and other rooms. Tropical trees and plants are fully integrated with the architecture, some of them growing up through specially positioned holes in the floor.

Colour elements are carefully used on the house's exterior. This neon pink wall highlights the top of the staircase. An outdoor kitchen area means that life can be lived in the sunshine. Stainless steel is an ideal material for this often humid space. The living room is simply decorated with generously sized furnishings: a white sofa, a red lacquer table, and a pink wall that matches the one outside.

Sharp colours are also found in the bedrooms and bathrooms: acid green or turquoise blue for the four-poster beds, and more turquoise for the outer wall of the bathroom. The floor is laid with broad grey tiles that are easy to clean, a perfect fit for the relaxed style of the house.

Welcoming shade is created with black Venetian blinds that shelter the interior from the strongest Caribbean sunlight. The house stays cool through natural ventilation: its broad open spaces create refreshing currents of air. The bedrooms have magnificent views out over the garden to the sea.

The bedrooms and bathrooms are colour-coded: blue for guests, green for the owners. The beds are hung with mosquito nets, a stylish but practical touch.

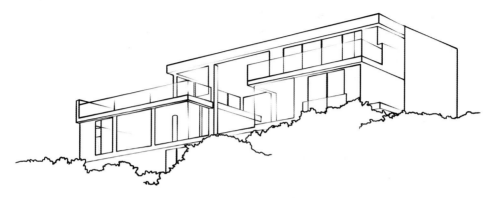

Contemporary Houses

An imaginative use of concrete is a particular feature of the houses in this section. The architects have taken full advantage of the malleable qualities of this material to create organic structures: walls that look like solid sails, for example, and twisted spaces that are reminiscent of a snail shell. White tends to dominate the interior and exterior spaces, as so often in hot climates. Whether it is the interplay of colours and materials at the house in Sydney, or the curving shapes of the house in Mexico, the architects have pushed their creativity to the limit. The use of modern materials does not make these buildings any less functional or pleasant to live in. The house in Sydney contains a small inner courtyard that serves to ventilate the rooms on hot days. Small windows and a semi-open living room at the house in Mexico help to keep indoor temperatures down all year round.

This house in Sydney, Australia, stays cool in the searing heat despite its large windows thanks to an internal courtyard that ventilates the interior spaces.

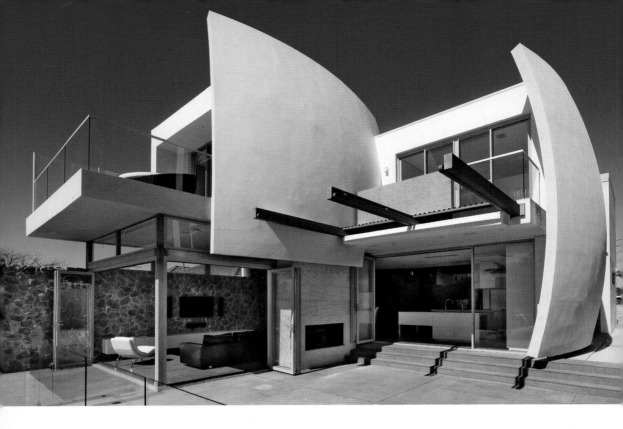

Bills House, Sydney, Australia

Tony Owen Partners designed this house for an industrialist whose company, specializing in concrete, took charge of the construction. It takes its inspiration from Mediterranean forms, with the curved concrete 'sails' of the exterior walls evoking Greek fishing boats.

The idea behind the house, located in a homogeneous suburban setting, was to create a sense of balance and minimize the impact on the environment as much as possible. The house consists of a series of internal levels which gradually step up from the road.

Tony Owen Partners

Established in Sydney in 2004, Tony Owen Partners has grown rapidly to become a mid-sized practice with a focus on a conceptual approach to commercial projects. The practice offers architectural, interiors and urban planning services. It has built several private luxury residences with swimming pools in Australia, using mainly concrete and glass, as well as numerous apartment blocks, institutional buildings such as stadiums, opera houses and synagogues.

BELOW This light, airy, modern house is characterized by a creative interplay of spaces, natural light and the rich nuances of the construction materials, which include polished and painted concrete, natural stone and wood.

OPPOSITE The black polished concrete staircase looks like a sculpture from various vantage points within the house. The dark material contrasts with the rest of the house, which is mainly decorated in white and natural shades.

The dominant features of the house are the curved, sail-like white walls, which cut through space and dematerialize the house. Large picture windows dissolve the boundaries between the internal and external spaces. The house is built around a large, sculptural staircase in dark polished concrete which connects the various level changes, and an interior courtyard to the west of the building which bathes the inner spaces in natural light and breaks up the façade. The kitchen and lounge-style living area merge with a large external space, which also contains the swimming pool with glass surround.

The living area with its natural stone wall and numerous windows overlooking the suburban landscape projects into the garden. A stream of light penetrates the interior, and the solid and hollow parts of the façade create an effective interplay of light and shadow.

The polished concrete interior with clean, geometric lines is furnished in a minimalist style. Great care has been taken over the artificial lighting, which is subdued. The dark door and window frames, floors, and even some of the furniture all match the black staircase, which is the central feature of the interior. A natural stone wall adds texture to the living room and softens the monolithic character of the building.

In the bathroom, the floor, walls and bathtub surround are all made of wood, creating a touch of warmth that contrasts with the starker feel of the other surfaces.

Forest Shell, Punta Ixtapa, Mexico

With its organic volumes, this large house resembles a shell rising out of the sand. The semi-open living room, which is shaded by the roof, has views of the ocean and the luxuriant vegetation surrounding the house.

Set on a private beach at Punta Ixtapa, a Mexican resort overlooking the Pacific Ocean, this spacious holiday home was designed for a large family by LAR/ Fernando Romero. In a traditional open-sided Mexican beach house, a number of wooden columns support a high thatched roof, which helps to ventilate the interior. This house takes a similar approach. Instead of columns, two organic volumes containing utility rooms and the master bedroom support the structure and provide privacy from the outside world. These two volumes are divided by a narrow entrance that leads to a large semi-open living area with magnificent views of the sea. The first floor, shaped like a shell, contains eight bedrooms, a kitchen and further living spaces. The decor is characterized by the use of plants and other organic materials.

LAR/Fernando Romero

Fernando Romero is a Mexican architect and entrepreneur. In 1998 he founded LAR (Laboratory of Architecture), with the goal of focusing on sustainable architectural solutions. He aims to offer his clients a reappropriation of space, an exploration of new geometric forms, and an innovative use of new materials. He is also the founder of Don Casa, a project that offers financial support to people from disadvantaged backgrounds, allowing them to build their own homes. In setting up this enterprise, Romero wanted to give an underprivileged section of the population the chance to become homeowners, while calling on the skills of local craftspeople and designers. His agency has won several awards for its innovative designs, particularly in the USA.

OPPOSITE A white path cuts through the lush garden. The tropical vegetation provides welcome shade in a country where temperatures can soar.

The thatched roof is made of palm leaves, in the traditional style of palapas. The house was designed with the warm climate in mind: both the open-plan ground floor and the palm roof facilitate natural ventilation and avoid the need for air conditioning. The small windows on the first floor help to shelter the interior from the sun.

Whitewashed reinforced concrete was used to build the house. The interior design is kept simple owing to the extravagant architecture: the only furniture on display is modern and white. The house embodies the search for architectural simplicity and fundamental purity.

ABOVE Continuing the cool feel of the interior, the staircase leads to the first floor, and the front-facing children's bedrooms and guest quarters.

Home in the Dunes, José Ignacio, Uruguay

Granite fireplaces and a pergola-covered open-air living and dining space provide structure to the fully glazed front elevation.

Situated 10 km (6 miles) from the small, chic seaside resort of José Ignacio, this house is built on dunes overlooking the Atlantic Ocean. The house has a surface area of 900 sq m (10,000 sq ft), and 12,500 sq m (135,000 sq ft) of grounds. The owners, an Argentinian couple with two children, wanted a house they could invite friends to in the summer, and so they called on Uruguayan architects Martin Gomez and Gonzalez Veloso. The property comprises five separate volumes and five suites, each with its own fireplace, living room, dining room, games room and home cinema.

Concrete

Concrete is a building material made from a mixture of cement, aggregate (such as sand and crushed gravel) and water which hardens to form a stone-like mass. Its properties can be adjusted by adding minerals or chemical admixtures.

> The quality of concrete depends not only on its ingredients but also on the way it is mixed, transported and used. Among its many benefits, concrete is very economical, is good at withstanding compressive forces, and is resistant to fire and chemical attack. On the other hand, it does not withstand tensile forces well, and as a result it is often reinforced with materials of high tensile strength such as steel.

> Various ancient civilizations used concrete for construction, including the Romans, but it was not until the second half of the 20th century and the reconstruction after the Second World War that its use became widespread. Concrete paved the way for new architectural forms and is now made into any shape imaginable by architects and engineers.

BELOW Some of the rooms, including the bedrooms, project out of the façade, in order to maximize the view of the ocean and the lighthouse that has given its name to the region.

OPPOSITE A large rectangular swimming pool with jacuzzi takes pride of place in the garden, which is filled with endemic species.

The house has a concrete structure. The exterior is clad with wood from the lapacho tree, which was held sacred by the Incas and prized primarily for its medicinal properties. Cedar panels clad the interior, which also features exposed concrete ceilings and large cement tiles on the floor. There are several outdoor seating areas for relaxation. The large swimming pool includes a jacuzzi for use all year round. A viewing platform in the grounds offers magnificent views of the beach and the surrounding landscape. It is surmounted by a small wooden watch house painted with black and white stripes.

In an ode to modern materials, the owners used concrete to make a statement. The concrete ceilings and supporting pillars have been left exposed to evoke the wild areas of countryside that still exist along the coast. Large cement tiles cover the floors.

Everything is geared to outdoor living: after an aperitif beneath the lapacho pergola, fish are cooked over an open-air grill and enjoyed at one of the exterior seating areas. All the external grills and internal fireplaces are made of locally sourced granite. The fireplace in the living room opens onto the lounge on one side and the dining room on the other. The kitchen has cedar wood panelling, stainless steel work surfaces, dark wicker pendant lamp shades and a marble table by Carrare. The bedrooms project out from the building and are furnished luxuriously in predominantly dark wood and leather.

Each room has cedar wood panelling, creating a cosy feel. The large rooms are furnished with a rich array of exquisite furniture. The turquoise tiles of the bathroom pictured below contrast with the natural shades that predominate in the rest of the house to create a pleasing effect.

The garden was designed to respect the natural topography and local vegetation, which includes acacias, tamarisks and pampas grass. Evenly spaced discs of lapacho slats form a path to the private beach.

Inside the house, the decor has been chosen with care. Items of furniture from various different periods and countries stand side by side: French chairs in the style of Louis XV and Louis XVI are arranged around a white Chinese table, alongside 20th-century chairs by the American designer Eero Saarinen. Add to this the Moroccan lamps and Asian furniture and the result is a rich mix of the old and the new.

Appendices

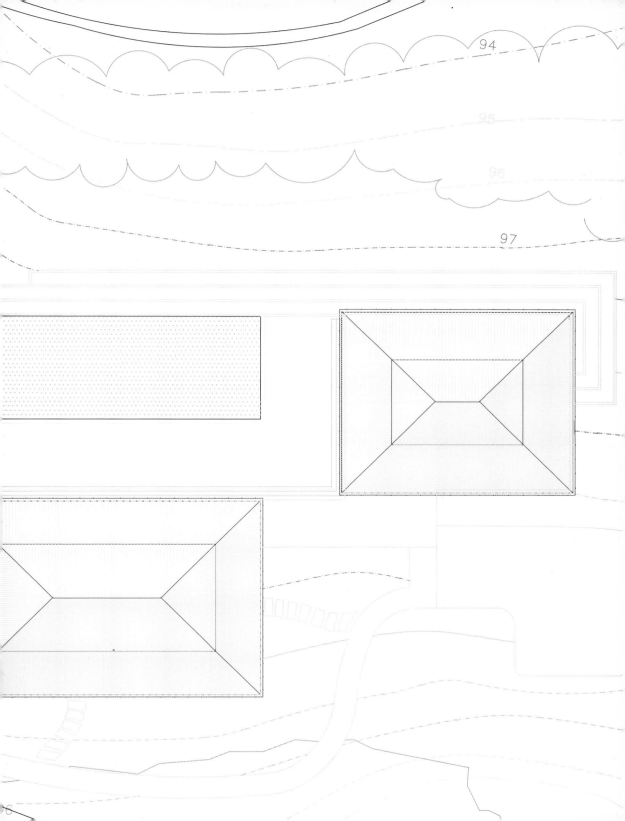

94

95

96

97

Glossary

• *Bateig*
A type of natural limestone tile, originating from Spain. It is fairly hardwearing and suitable for interior walls or floors.

• *Canal tiles*
Also known as barrel tiles, or mission tiles, these are semi-circular roof tiles that are laid to form alternating ridges and channels. They are particularly common in the south of France and other Mediterranean regions.

• *Cantilever*
A construction element based around a beam that is supported at only one end. Common uses of cantilevers include overhanging balconies and corbels.

• *Corian*
A trademark of the DuPont company, Corian is a solid surface material made from a blend of acrylic polymer and natural minerals. Non-porous and available in a range of colours, it can be used for kitchen and bathroom surfaces, sinks, wall cladding and more.

• *Epoxy resin*
A polymer resin commonly used in plastics, adhesives and coatings.

• *Itaúba wood*
A tropical hardwood whose botanical name is *Mezilaurus itauba*. Tough and hardwearing, it is used for timber frame construction as well as furniture.

• *Palapa*
A traditional Mexican shelter with open sides and a roof of palm leaves or branches.

• *Polished concrete*
A decorative surface that is produced by treating concrete with a hardener and then grinding it to a high sheen.

• *Post-and-beam framing*
A method of timber construction based around a framework of horizontal beams supported by vertical posts.

• *Sustainable architecture*
Also known as green architecture or eco-architecture, this term covers building practices that are designed to minimize environmental impact.

Directory of Architects

• *Javier Artadi/Artadi Arquitectos*
Camino Real 111 Of. 701 San Isidro
Lima, Peru
www.javierartadi.com

• *Walter F. Chatham Architect*
55 Crosby Street, 1
New York City 10012, USA
www.wfchatham.com

• *Simon Conder Associates Ltd*
Architects + Designers
Nile Street Studios
8 Nile Street
London N1 7RF, UK
www.simonconder.co.uk

• *José Forjaz Arquitectos*
Av. 24 de Julho, 67
Maputo, Mozambique
www.joseforjazarquitectos.com

• *Grandberg & Associates Architects*
117 East Main Street
Mount Kisco, NY 10549, USA
www.grandbergarchitects.com

• *Marcio Kogan/Studio MK27*
Alameda Tiête, 505
Cerqueira César
São Paulo, SP, Brazil
www.marciokogan.com.br

• *LAR/Fernando Romero*
Mexico: Gral. Francisco Ramirez 5,
Mexico City
USA: 511 West 25th St, 911,
New York, NY 10001
www.lar-fr.com

• *MacKay-Lyons Sweetapple Architects Ltd*
2188 Gottingen Street
Halifax, Nova Scotia
Canada B3K 3B4
www.mlsarchitects.ca

• *Pascal Morabito*
16 Place Vendôme
75001 Paris, France
www.pascalmorabito.com

• *Morabito Art Villa*
Berawa Beach Street, Canggu
80361 Kuta Utara,
Bali, Indonesia
www.morabitoartvilla.com

• *Tony Owen Partners*
Architects Planners Interiors
Level 2, 12–16 Queen Street
Chippendale, New South Wales, 2008
Australia
www.tonyowen.com.au

• *Rost Niderehe Architekten – Ingenieure*
Uferstrasse 8C
22081 Hamburg, Germany
www.rost-niderehe.de

Further Reading

Bradbury, Dominic, *Mediterranean Modern*, London and New York: Thames & Hudson, 2006

Campbell, James W. P., photographs by Will Pryce, *Brick: A World History*, London and New York: Thames & Hudson, 2003

Cliff, Stafford, and Gilles de Chabaneix, *The Way We Live: Making Homes / Creating Lifestyles*, London: Thames & Hudson, 2003

Dos Santos, Solvi, *Baltic Homes: Inspirational Interiors from Northern Europe*, London: Thames & Hudson, 2005

Invernizzi Tettoni, Luca, *Ultimate Tropical*, London: Thames & Hudson, 2008, and New York: Rizzoli, 2009

Klimi, Julia, *At Home in Greece*, London and New York: Thames & Hudson, 2004

Listri, Massimo, *Casa Mundi: Inspirational Living from around the World*, London: Thames & Hudson, 2008

Listri, Massimo, *Casa Mediterranea: Spectacular Houses and Glorious Gardens by the Sea*, London and New York: Thames & Hudson, 2009

McMillian, Elizabeth Jean, *Living on the Water*, London: Thames & Hudson and New York: Rizzoli, 1998

Magnago Lampugnani, Vittorio (ed.), *The Thames & Hudson Dictionary of 20th-Century Architecture*, 'World of Art' series, London: Thames & Hudson, 1986

Mathewson, Casey C. M., *Residential Designs for the 21st Century: An International Collection*, Willowdale, Ont.: Firefly, 2007

Norberg-Schulz, Christian, *Existence, Space & Architecture*, London: Studio Vista, 1971

The Phaidon Atlas of 21st Century World Architecture, London: Phaidon, 2008

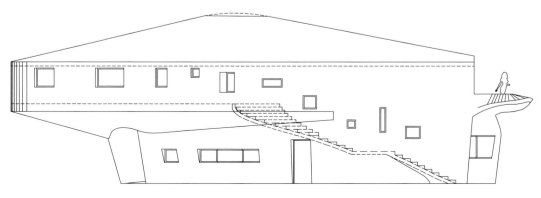

© LAR / Fernando Romero

Acknowledgments

The author would like to thank Catherine Laulhère-Vigneau for entrusting this project to her. She would also like to thank Céline Adida for her patience and professionalism throughout the creation of this book, which would not have been possible without her help. Thanks also to Marie Peyronnet for her elegant design and thoughtful comments, to James Elliott, to the Hemis.fr picture agency, and to all the architectural practices which took part.

The publisher and the author would also like to thank all the architects whose work appears in this book: Javier Artadi and Miluzka Vásquez Diaz from Artadi Arquitectos; Tony Owen and Esan Rahmani from Tony Owen Partners; Marcio Kogan, Marian Simas, Suzana Glogowski, Diana Radomysler and Carolina Castroviejo from Studio MK27; Walter F. Chatham; José Forjaz and Jorge Campos from José Forjaz Arquitectos; Pascal Morabito, Marie-Êve and Teo from Morabito; Simon Conder and Ayesha Wynne from Simon Conder Associates; Ira Grandberg and Craig Intimarelli from Grandberg & Associates; Fernando Romero and Susana Hernández Aparicio from LAR; Sawa Rostkowska from MacKay-Lyons Sweetapple Architects; Jorg Niderehe and Amélie Rost from Rost Niderehe; Claire Chamot; Constance Parpoil; Renaud Lopin.

Picture Credits

a = above, b = below, c = centre, l = left, r = right: Felipe Branquinho for José Forjaz Arquitectos 182, 183 a, 183 b, 184, 185, 186, 187; Dan Gair/Blind Dog Photo Inc for Walter Chatham 102, 103 a, 103 b, 104 a, 104 b, 105 al, 105 cl, 105 bl, 105 ar, 105 cr, 105 br; Chris Gascoigne for Simon Conder Associates 65 b, 66 a, 66 b, 69; Luis Gordoa for LAR/Fernando Romero 202, 205 r; Hemis.fr/Serge Anton 189 a, 189 b, 190, 191, 192 l, 192 b, 193; Hemis.fr/Jon Arnold 214 br, 215 bl; Hemis.fr/Franco Barbagallo 214 al; Hemis.fr/Emmanuel Berthier 7 ar, 163 b; Hemis.fr/Philippe Body 11 b; Hemis.fr/Christophe Boisvieux 4, 12, 13, 28; Hemis.fr/Serge Brison 126, 128, 129 a, 130, 131, 132, 133 al, 133 bl, 133 ar, 133 br; Hemis.fr/Bieke Claessens 22, 23, 24, 25 l, 25 ca, 25 cb, 25 ar, 25 br, 26 al, 26 bl, 26 ar, 26 br, 27, 34, 35, 36 bl, 36 br, 37, 38, 39 al, 39 bl, 39 ar, 39 br, 70b, 134, 135, 136, 137 l, 137 ar, 137 br, 138, 139 (all images); Hemis.fr/Jean-Pierre Degas 74; Hemis.fr/Solvi Dos Santos 10 a, 30, 31, 32 al, 32 cl, 32 bl, 32 ar, 32 cr, 33, 40, 41, 42, 43 al, 43 bl, 43 ac, 43 bc, 43 ar, 43 br, 46, 47 a, 47 bl, 47 br, 48, 49 al, 49 ar, 49 b, 50, 51 (all images), 52 al, 52 bl, 52 ar, 52 cr, 52 br, 53, 71 a, 76, 77 (all images), 78, 79, 80 al, 80 ar, 80 b, 81 al, 81 bl, 81 bc, 81 ar, 81 br, 82, 83, 84, 85 al, 85 ac, 85 ar, 85 b, 86 a, 86 b, 87 a, 87 bl, 87 br, 108 l, 108 r, 109 a, 110 al, 110 bl, 110 ar, 110 br, 111, 112 al, 112 bl, 112 ar, 112 br, 113 al, 113 bl, 113 ar, 113 br; Hemis.fr/Marc Dozier 214 bl; Hemis.fr/Mezza Escalante 206, 207 a, 207 b, 208 (all images), 209, 210, 211 a, 211 b, 212, 213 al, 213 bl, 213 ac, 213 bc, 213 ar, 213 br; Hemis.fr/Stéphane Frances 198; Hemis.fr/Bertrand Gardel 10 b, 215 br; Hemis.fr/Franck Guiziou 106, 214 ar; Hemis.fr/Nick Guttridge 129 b; Hemis.fr/Martin Hahn and Micky Hoyle 98 l, 98 r, 99 al, 99 ar, 99 bl, 99 bc, 99 br, 100, 101 l, 101 r; Hemis.fr/Christian Heeb 150; Hemis.fr/Micky Hoyle 72, 120 l, 120 r, 121, 122, 123 al, 123 bl, 123 ac, 123 bc, 123 ar, 124, 125 al, 125 bl, 125 ac, 125 bc, 125 ar; Hemis.fr/Imagebroker 71 b; Hemis.fr/Hartmut Krinitz 7 cl, 44; Hemis.fr/René Mattes 70 a; Hemis.fr/Miaoulis 7 br, 88, 89 al, 89 bl, 89 ar, 89 br, 90, 91 al, 91 bl, 91 ac, 91 bc, 91 ar, 92, 94, 95 al, 95 cl, 95 bl, 95 ar, 95 cr, 95 br, 96 a, 96 b, 97 al, 97 bl, 97 ar, 97 br; Hemis.fr/Bruno Morandi 215 cl; Hemis.fr/Thomas Patrice 215 al; Hemis.fr/Pierce/Photoshot 7 bl, 214 cl, 215 cr; Hemis.fr/Philippe Renault 148; Hemis.fr/Bertrand Rieger 7 al, 214 cr, 215 ar; Hemis.fr/Gilles Rigoulet 36 a; Hemis.fr/Robert Harding Picture Library 64; Hemis.fr/Mireille Roobaert 166, 170 a, 170 b, 171 al, 171 bl, 171 br; Hemis.fr/Christian Sarramon 14, 16, 17, 18 a, 18 b, 18 r, 19, 20 l, 20 r, 21; Hemis.fr/Annette Soumillard 144 b; Hemis.fr/Dominique Vorillon 7 cr, 145, 151 a, 151 bl, 151 bc, 151 br, 152 a, 152 b, 153 al, 153 bl, 153 ac, 153 bc, 153 ar, 154, 155, 156 a, 156 b, 157 al, 157 bl, 157 ac, 157 bc, 157 ar, 157 br, 158, 160, 161 a, 161 b, 162 al, 162 bl, 162 ar, 162 br, 163 al, 163 ar, 164 a, 164 bl, 164 br, 165; Nelson Kon for Marcio Kogan/Studio MK27 172, 173 a, 173 b, 174 (all images), 175; Jens Kroell for Rost Niderehe 55 a, 56, 57 a, 57 b; Renaud Lopin 73, 114, 115 a, 115 bl, 115 br, 116 a, 116 b, 117 l, 117 r, 118 al, 118 ar, 118 b, 119; Brian MacKay-Lyons for MacKay-Lyons Sweetapple 61 a, 61 b; Pascal Morabito 167 a, 167 b, 168, 169 a, 169 b, 171 ar; Tony Owen/Earlwood for Tony Owen Partners 194, 196, 197 a, 197 b, 198, 199 al, 199 bl, 199 ar, 199 br; Tony Patterson (drawing) for MacKay-Lyons Sweetapple 59; Marie Peyronnet (drawings) 5, 6, 15, 29, 45, 75, 93, 107, 127, 149, 159, 177, 195, 237; Marie Peyronnet 53 b, 109 b; Greg Richardson for MacKay-Lyons Sweetapple 58, 62, 63 al, 63 b, 63 ar; Amelie Rost for Rost Niderehe 54, 55 b; Raoul Manuel Schnell for MacKay-Lyons Sweetapple 60; Jorge Silva for LAR/Fernando Romero 203 a, 203 b; Paul Smoothy for Simon Conder Associates 65 a, 67, 68; Jan Staller for Grandberg & Associates 140, 141 a, 141 b, 142, 143 al, 143 bl, 143 ar, 143 br; Adam Wiseman for LAR/Fernando Romero 204, 205 l

Translated from the French *Maisons des Bords de Mer* by Rebekah Wilson

First published in the United Kingdom in 2011 by
Thames & Hudson Ltd, 181A High Holborn,
London WC1V 7QX

www.thamesandhudson.com

First published in 2011 in paperback in the United States of America by
Thames & Hudson Inc., 500 Fifth Avenue, New York, New York 10110

thamesandhudsonusa.com

Original edition © 2011 Éditions Glénat, Grenoble
This edition © 2011 Thames & Hudson Ltd, London

British Library Cataloguing-in-Publication Data
A catalogue record for this book is available from the British Library

Library of Congress Catalog Card Number 2011922606

ISBN: 978-0-500-28962-4

Printed and bound in China by Book Partners China Ltd

There be Dragons

Heather Graham

Illustrated by

Cherif Fortin & Lynn Sanders

Bonus CD produced by

Reuwen Amiel

Medallion Press
Masterpiece Collection

Published 2009 by Medallion Press, Inc.

The MEDALLION PRESS LOGO
is a registered trademark of Medallion Press, Inc.

Copyright © 2009 by Heather Graham
Artwork by Cherif Fortin and Lynn Sanders
Cover design by Adam Mock and James Tampa
Book design by James Tampa
Bonus CD produced by Reuven Amiel
Costumes by Connie Perry

Printed in the United States of America
Typeset in Adobe Garamond Pro

Library of Congress Cataloging-in-Publication Data

Graham, Heather.
  There be dragons / Heather Graham.
    p. cm.
  ISBN 978-1-60542-071-4
  I. Title.
  PS3557.R198T54 2009
  813'.54--dc22
                              2009005945

10 9 8 7 6 5 4 3 2 1
First Edition

ACKNOWLEDGMENTS:

To all those who made this such a fun and wonderful project, Bryee-Annon, Chynna, Jason, Shayne, and Derek Pozzessere, Yevgeniya Yeretskaya-Pozzessere, Helen and James Rosburg, Ali DeGray, Patric Falcon, Abdiel Vivancos, D.J. and Graham Davant, Franci Naulin, Teresa Davant, Al Perry, Alicia Ibarra, Bobby and Victoria Sophia Rosello, and very especially Lynn Sanders, Cherif Fortin, Reuven Amiel, and Connie Perry.

Young
Michelo

Nico d'Or

Michelo

Marina

Geovana

Fiorelli

Lendo

Baristo

d'Artois

Daphne

Prologue
Legends

Once upon a time, before the world of man was as old as it is today—but after it was as young as it might have been—there was a beautiful land called Calasia, caught between the new age of logic and the ancient days of magic. It was ruled by the great Duke Fiorelli, and beneath him, in power in their feudal lands, were two renowned warrior counts, the lords of Lendo and Baristo. Calasia, governed by the great Duke Fiorelli, prospered, laws were just, and art and music were loved and enjoyed.

But to the south lived the fierce People of the Distant Land, and when they threatened the borders of Calasia, three great warriors, the leaders of the land, went out to meet them. It had been some time since such an enemy had been met, and those who went rode to fight hard indeed, for it was said their enemies had among their ranks a group of great, tall, dreaded wargnomes, beings said to have armored skin, reptilian scales that gave them the ability to defy the swords and arrows of mortal warriors.

Hectobar, one of the horrid battle lords who led the enemy forces, was known to have stolen a princess from a nearby realm. Being gallant knights, the noblemen of Calasia would not only protect their borders, but they would not stop until they had freed the beautiful damsel in distress. So they rode, and a great battle ensued.

In the midst of the fighting, Alphonso, Count of Lendo, was caught in a tight arena of terrible combat. He could not be reached by his old and dear friend, Fiorelli, and later, the Count of Baristo would claim he was too far from the fighting to go to Alphonso's aid. And so it was that Nico d'Or, falcon master to the Count, came into the picture. Brave and courageous, he rode forward, fought relentlessly, and smote the enemy to free the Count of Lendo from the evil hordes surrounding him. But alas, the Count of Lendo had received a mortal blow, and in the arms of his falcon master, he found his last strength and comfort. He commended the keeping of Lendo to Nico d'Or, the falcon master, who had proven his strength and loyalty.

As the Count of Lendo placed all he held dear in d'Or's keeping and sighed his last breath, Nico d'Or rose with a great heartache and a roar of fury, swearing the fine old count would not die in vain.

The knights of Calasia joined in his rage, rallied, and rode on with great speed. They came upon the horrid creature Hectobar, who still held the feisty princess. So great was d'Or's fury, he hopped atop the creature Hectobar, and, with his bare hands, strangled the beast.

The princess, Elisia, impressed by the mighty knight who had saved her, had no desire to be returned to her home. The great Duke Fiorelli thought it was only natural that the princess be granted to the brave falcon master, Nico d'Or, and that the brave fellow indeed be given the lands and title of Lendo. This was an easy ruling for the great Duke Fiorelli, for he was a married man himself, with a lovely duchess who had given him a fine and hearty son for an heir, as well as a lovely daughter.

Now, it should have been quite acceptable to Marco, Count of Baristo, as well, for he, too, had a countess, Geovana, and a son. However, it was rumored his wife was a witch. She had come from the dark lands to the northeast of the lovely peninsula on which they all lived. Many believed that if his wife *was* indeed a witch, it was entirely his own fault. The Count of Baristo was an ambitious man, fond of fine living and improving his own holdings, and he was disgruntled. The falcon master was given a beautiful, sweet, wealthy bride, and he was returning home to . . .

Well, his not so sweet, lovely, or wealthy bride.

Despite his displeasure, there was nothing the Count of Baristo could do, except, of course, return home to his countess, Geovana, where the poor man discovered his wife was far more unhappy than he!

Furious that he had not been the one to rush to the aid of the Count of Lendo, she added to his woes. Had he done so, the charming village and rich and fertile lands of Lendo might have been granted to him, rather than being bestowed upon—of all people!—the falcon master. (To add to Geovanna's disappointment, certain rumors reached her regarding her own husband, namely that he, too, had been quite infatuated with the rescued princess, Elisia.)

However pleased or not pleased as they might be, Nico d'Or was to marry Elisia.

The night of the formal wedding announcement, Geovana's servants heard her upon the balcony. Dressed in the black she chose for just such occasions of dark and deadly mood, she stood outside, reaching upward to the sky, chanting. Her voice rose and fell in a strange and uncanny sound of fury. Her cries rose with a vengeance. There was a terrible storm that night, and many thought the sound was the whipping of the wind and the crackle and boom of the thunder.

Long after midnight, the Countess at last came in, calm and serene, and strangely pleasant to all those around her. The people marveled that she had, it seemed, realized the wealth of her own position, and the blessings of her son and husband.

The next morning was when the dragon appeared.

It was beautiful in its wickedness, royal purple and midnight black in color, winged and frilled, with huge dark eyes, a shimmering long tail, and a sharply pointed spine.

The day was rough, with lightning flashing again and again, and storm clouds sweeping the sun away. Some thought they imagined the creature, but when the princess Elisia came to stand upon the balcony at Lendo, dressed in her wedding finery, the dragon came down and swept her away.

It was quite odd that—when she heard the news—Geovana, along with her cries of, "Oh, no!" and "Oh, dear!"—appeared to be either secretly smiling or smirking.

Nico d'Or, the new Count of Lendo, was distraught, and followed a trail, it is said, of blue smoke. The trail took him high upon the cliffs, where great crags and caves were in abundance. He had gone alone in his haste and desperation that no harm should come to his princess, his only weapons a sword and strength of will.

Legend says it was pureness within his heart, along with his fear for the life of another, that led him straight to the dragon. Though he did not see the creature die, he was certain he had inflicted a mortal injury upon the beast. At the least, he wrested his princess free.

In Lendo, all rejoiced. The wedding would be that night, as planned.

But that very same night, the Countess of Baristo apparently suffered a fall or some injury. Still, she was determined to attend the wedding. She dragged herself from her sickbed. For the occasion, she even doffed her habitual black shade of dress, and arrived in shining white in honor of the pair. After the ceremony, she kindly cast a spell for the newlyweds, one that granted love and happiness for all the time they might have together.

As a married couple, Elisia and d'Or were happy. Deeply happy, deeply in love.

Indeed, Geovana had cast such a spell. She neglected to tell the couple, of course, that her spell had included the fact that their happy time together would not last more than a decade.

Life went on. Elisia and Nico, Lady and Lord of Lendo, found happiness in themselves, and though they rued the lack of a child, they worked hard for those around them.

In time, however, they were distressed to hear about the death of their neighbor, the Count of Baristo. They sent their deepest condolences to the Countess Geovana, and sent servants with food and priests to pray for the dear deceased's soul. The Countess, however, was inconsolable (many said, "Rot!"), and though none knew why, she blamed the happy couple for the death of her husband. Many thought her grief quite exaggerated, for it was whispered that the two had argued most vociferously, and that even the stone walls of the castle were known to shiver by night.

However, in the wondrous haven of Lendo, Elisia and Nico lived in a delightful world of love and peace. The only thing lacking was a child, the deepest desire of both Elisia and her count.

Then a baby girl was at last born to the couple. She was called Marina, for her parents both so dearly loved the sea.

The rejoicing in Lendo was quite incredible, because the people lived in such peace and harmony. There were so many gifts! Beautiful gifts! Most of them.

The Countess Geovana of Baristo sent a rather unusual present. It was quite lovely, but rather large for a tiny infant. It was a bed, beautifully carved, with a soft mattress and elegant silk and velvet trappings. It came with the suggestion that her son and their daughter should become betrothed, and marry at the appropriate time.

Now Nico and Elisia had become well aware by that time that the Countess Geovana did not always intend the best for others. As politely as they could, they hemmed and hawed and suggested they must let the children grow older, and see if they were at all compatible. Geovana seemed to accept their words; she smiled, and raised a glass to them, and murmured something beneath her breath. She touched the bed, and oddly, upon the elegant trappings, she set a stone. All for luck, of course, she told them, and it was only later, late at night, sleeping by the side of his lady, that Nico d'Or remembered that luck could be good—and quite bad, and so he removed the stone from the bed.

For a few years more, all was a most wondrous fantasy in Lendo. Then . . . tragedy.

The Count awoke one morning feeling fine. That night, however, a storm rose. It was said that the wind had the sound of a woman's screams. The good Count d'Or went among the villagers, helping them gather their livestock into the safety of the walls. And as they came through an archway, a stone fell, striking the Count on the head.

His countess raced through the driving rain. She wrapped him tenderly in her arms. The finest physicians were called, the greatest wizards. But all to no avail.

The brave and kindly count departed his wondrous world. As he died, the clock struck twelve, and seemed to toll out a misery all its own. At the last stroke, the sky, cleared then of the rain, was filled with stars that created the shape of a magnificent, flying steed. Some of the people found peace in the beautiful sight, for they believed that the Count, risen from the status of falcon master, had found his soul borne away by magical wings, and flown in such a soaring fashion to heaven.

Elisia was inconsolable. But Duke Fiorelli came to see her when an appropriate time had passed, telling her that she must marry again, for the People of the Distant Land were ever ready to ride hard and take what they could. She mentioned to him that Count Baristo's widow had not remarried, and even the great Fiorelli was perplexed. He was loathe to admit to the sweet and beautiful Elisia that he knew of few knights or noblemen brave enough to wed the Countess Baristo.

In time, it was arranged. And it was actually through the Countess Geovana that Elisia met the Count d'Artois, a handsome man from the Place of Misty Mountains and Legends, where Geovana herself had been raised. He had a daughter near the age of Elisia's own dear Marina. (Some thought it strange that Geovana had not sought out this knight for herself; others noted that Geovana often had ever-so-slightly devious long-range plans.)

And so, once again, wedding bells rang out and pealed across the hills and cliffs of Lendo.

People came from far and wide. All rejoiced, and it seemed that even the Countess Geovana was at peace, for she arrived once more dressed in splendid white, bearing many gifts (that were actually quite normal gifts, silver and plate). She danced and laughed at the ceremony, and she was, in fact, so charming and lovely that Duke Fiorelli began to believe he might, after all, find the widow a new husband.

In Lendo then, it seemed, there would be peace and strength and prosperity, until . . .

Once again, a storm rose. And it was quite bizarre, for the Countess Elisia was sleeping in her own bed when a stone flew straight into the bedroom, borne on the wind. It struck her on the head.

Within a fortnight, she, too, passed away. She did so as had her dearly beloved Nico, at the stroke of twelve. When the clock echoed with its last chime, the heavens cleared again and the stars formed the shape of a magnificent, magical falcon. The people whispered that her soul had been taken through the stars to join with Nico's. True or not, it made for a lovely legend.

Lendo was cast into a deep mourning, for Elisia had been so dearly adored by her people.

The talk around the countryside became, with the passage of time, quite practical. Thank goodness that the Countess had remarried, for Lendo was, at least, left with a new lord.

There was always danger on the wind. The People of a Distant Land might send raiders again at any time.

And then again, they did, indeed, live in a time of dragons . . .

Years passed.

Fire and danger forever threatened.

Even when the beauty of peace of Christmastide came near.

Return to a Time of Magic

Chapter 1

Marina was awakened by a thumping sound in the back courtyard below her window. She rose quickly, and walked to look out.

And there he was.

Armand, out before the dawn, battling it out with the scarecrow.

Unfortunately, it appeared that the scarecrow was winning. Armand was clad in mail, mask down on his helm. Apparently, he'd been on his horse, Ares, practicing with his sword against the dummy set in the yard, a place where all the fighting men and knights might hone their skills at thrusting hard against the enemy.

Armand had missed the scarecrow.

With his impetus, he had left his seat upon Ares.

His well-trained mount waited a distance from Armand, as if he was determined not to look at his master in his distress, and hopefully, save him any embarrassment. Armand was now sitting on his rear, hands upon the ground, shaking his head. A moment later, he lifted his visor, then removed his helmet, and saw his cousin looking down.

He scowled for a moment, then sighed. "Honestly, I believe that scarecrow moved!" he told Marina.

She gave him a warm smile, feeling a soft sigh in her own heart. Armand was so determined. "Give me a minute; I'm coming right down. Did you hurt yourself?"

He tried moving. "No—I'm afraid that my rear section is quite accustomed to hitting dirt," he said.

Marina turned from the window, caught up her cape, and came running down the spiral staircase to the back. Once, her room had been in front of the house d'Or, and her windows had overlooked the garden.

She scarcely remembered that time, and she didn't particularly care that she had been relegated to the rear, overlooking the practice courtyard. She enjoyed riding herself, and learning by all that she watched.

When she reached the courtyard, Armand was still dusting himself off. "Ares, are you sure we rode quite straight?" he demanded of his mount.

The huge horse, granted to him because of his status as falcon master, after his own uncle and then father, raised and lowered its handsome head, as if speaking to him in return and assuring him he had done his best.

"Armand, you're the finest rider I know. Honestly, there is no reason for you to become a great warrior."

"There is every reason," he assured her. He walked toward the well, drawing up the bucket and ladle and drinking thirstily. Marina followed him, and Ares ambled along, as well.

"Armand—"

"Marina, I can prove that I'm a worthy suitor for Daphne. I can make the Count d'Artois realize I am an incredible asset to him, and that I should be allowed to love his daughter." He started to say more, then hesitated. He set the ladle back in the water bucket and looked at Marina again. "He intends to have you both married off within a fortnight, you know." He made a face. "Christmas weddings. How lovely."

Marina gritted her teeth against the shudder that swept through her. Christmas. A time she loved so much, with carols in the air and the holly decorated with bows, mistletoe here and there, and all the pageantry. A time of peace and beauty. A time to be thankful.

For the young Count Carlo Baristo?

She shuddered and looked to the heavens; unable to prevent a moment in which she wasn't thankful at all, she wondered only, *Dear God, what are you thinking?*

"Well, that's the problem, isn't it?" she said aloud. "My stepfather is quite determined that Lendo, Baristo, and the lands of Fiorelli be cemented by blood."

"Ah, yes! And there you will be, wife of the great Carlo, Count Baristo!"

"And," she reminded him, "your precious Daphne is to be given over to Michelo Fiorelli. He, at least, is reputed to be handsome and gallant."

"Reputed to be so . . . I don't remember the last time we've seen him. Because he, of course," Armand added bitterly, "has been off fighting in the south, gallantly coming to the aid of nobles in distress wherever they may be."

"There has been a flare-up of trouble in the south," she reminded him, and added softly, "I remember my father saying we must always be strong at the borders of our world, and that we can never let enemies—such as wartrolls, wargnomes, and the People of the Distant Land—take an inch away from us, because they will then take a foot, a yard, an acre, and a village."

"All the more reason I must learn to do battle with a scarecrow," Armand said dolefully.

"But you can ride so beautifully," she told him. "And you have an ability with horses, hounds, hawks, and falcons that is surely a greater gift than you can imagine. You speak softly with such animals, and they listen."

He tousled her hair with affection. "Cousin, I don't speak *with* the animals, only *to* them, and draw from them obedience and loyalty because I earn their trust. Just as you do. Ah, well, we are both the offspring of falcon masters, eh? And we both have a gift with animals. Which, of course, if you truly marry Carlo Baristo, is a talent you may well need."

She stared at him. "Thank you so very much! As if this isn't all just as wretched as it can be to begin with!" She shuddered. "I cannot marry Carlo."

"He's not so bad. Many a village lass has been known to swoon at his passing."

"He has but one thought in mind."

Armand cleared his throat, slightly embarrassed. "Ah, yes. The duties of the bedchamber," he said solemnly.

"No!" she told him impatiently. "His thought is to rule all these lands, and he isn't at all stupid. He wishes to marry me, because I am the daughter of Nico and Elisia, and because my father and mother are remembered with such love and esteem. And naturally, my stepfather sees nothing wrong with this because his daughter will become a duchess, and Duke Fiorelli sees nothing wrong with this, because Daphne is beautiful and accomplished."

"So we are all in a sorry state," Armand said, and his tone was soft, indeed sorry, and somewhat bitter.

"Daphne thinks the world of you, I believe," Marina said.

"Do you dislike her so, then?" Armand asked. He shrugged. "I mean, she is the daughter of your stepfather. And you were pushed to the back of the house soon after she arrived, while she was given your lovely garden view."

"Don't be silly, Armand. I don't dislike Daphne. I barely know her. I mean, even after all this time. She is always . . . somewhere. Daphne must play the lute, she must dance, she must sing. We barely pass in the halls, so it seems." Her eyes narrowed. "I don't even dislike her silly father."

"Hush, fie on you!" he teased. "D'Artois may be listening. Many people believe that the old stone walls of this place have ears."

"It's her!" Marina said softly.

Armand arched a brow in surprise. "Her?"

"Geovana."

Armand studied his cousin for a moment. "Marina, you mustn't believe the old rumors. Geovana has always been kind to me, and I do believe she is concerned for the welfare of our land. She has seen so much happen . . . she lost her husband so long ago, and then her friends, your parents. And think on it—your stepfather isn't really a horrible sort, and she's the one who brought him here and introduced him to your mother."

"Armand! You may spend your days with horses, but you are as blind as a bat in sunlight. She is like a . . . wartroll."

"She can be quite kind and courteous."

"She is a witch. You will note; she is alive, while Elisia, my mother, is not! She is a witch."

"There is no such thing, not really. Witches, wizards, creatures of the dark . . . they are called such because, in our minds, we must come up with reasons that our enemies should conquer, and we should fail. We find we must say, 'It's magic; it's destiny.' And thus we deal with that which otherwise we cannot. Anyway, you should start to think of Geovana more kindly. She'll be your mother-in-law."

"I can't marry him," Marina said. "And stop smirking at me!"

"I am not smirking. I am being bitter with you. So, what will you do? Run away?"

"I believe we are part of the prosperity here in Lendo, that our family has kept the traditions, safety, and laws of the village . . . I couldn't leave. Who knows what might happen if none of us was here?"

Armand touched her on the chin. "Then you shall have to start calling Geovana 'Mother' soon, for it seems your stepfather and the Countess of Baristo are quite determined. And, by the way, if you wish to avoid your future mate, you might want to run back upstairs. He and his men will be arriving for their birds and horses quite soon—there's a hunt planned for this morning."

"Now you tell me, Armand! I wish to avoid him at all costs!"

She started back for the stairs, but even as she began to flee, the gates to the rear courtyard opened, and a group of men came walking in.

They came with long strides, clad in the colors of Baristo, and Marina thought they all walked alike, with stiff shoulders and a terrible swagger. She halted, for they were between her and the stairway, and she was certainly far too late to escape them.

Naturally, Carlo Baristo was at the head of the swains, beyond a doubt, the best swaggerer of the group. Tall and dark, he was a man in fine form, spending a great deal of his time battling scarecrows in the yard, and, true in his case, winning the battle each time against his immobile opponent.

He smiled when he saw her. There was something about his smile that made her uneasy. It was a *smarmy* smile at best. And then there was his *voice*. It might sound just fine to others, but Marina always felt the sound was like the tear of metal against metal. Then, of course, it could all simply be because she didn't like or trust the man.

"Ah, Marina, my dear. Will you be joining us, then?"

"No, I'm so sorry, I'm afraid I can't."

"Oh? And why not?"

She stared at him blankly. "Because . . . I must bring flowers to my parents' grave sites."

He arched a brow. "Marina, I'm so sorry to remind you, but your parents are dead. Surely, it will make little difference if you bring the flowers now—or later."

"Ah, but this is a vow I've made, you see, and therefore, I must."

"I'm certain your parents, known for their wisdom and compassion, would quite understand."

"But I would not, for the vow is in my heart. Perhaps I should remind you as well, I'm not particularly fond of the hunt."

"A falcon master's daughter, and not fond of the hunt!"

"I'm afraid not."

"And alas, I'm afraid the entire village is fond of eating, and my men and I do bring in the majority of the meat."

"Of course! No one has ever doubted your ability, my lord, to best the beasts in the forest with your arrows and knives. I've heard there is new fighting at the border, that the wartroll and People of the Distant Land have begun to encroach again. In fact, I've heard we never do see Fiorelli's son, Michelo, because he is in command of defenses there. With your incredible ability with weapons, we must all be grateful you are here, among us, fighting rabbits, and not risking life and limb at the border. Indeed, we all must eat. I am so sorry, forgive my blindness. As for today, forgive me again. I truly cannot accompany you. I am committed this morning. So, Carlo, if you'll be kind enough to excuse me . . ."

Marina started by him. A strong hand upon her arm curtailed what she hoped would be a swift departure. Her sarcasm, no matter how pleasantly spoken, had not been lost on him. He was angry. But then, beneath his pleasantries, it seemed he was angry most of the time.

"Marina, are you aware your stepfather, my mother, and the great Duke Fiorelli have quite agreed on the future of our three holdings—and the fate of our lives. You're to be my wife, which of course, pleases me to no end. A lovely, magnificent Christmas present. Since that is to be our destiny, perhaps we should spend more time together."

"I am committed this morning, Carlo."

He released her arm, yet his eyes pierced like daggers—which were they, as she often thought—she'd have been pinned to the spot. He lowered his head to speak with her. "In very little time, my dear, you will truly be committed."

"I really must go."

"Straight to the grave?"

Was it a threat? Or was he simply questioning her intent?

Thankfully, her cloak was all-encompassing. He could have no idea that she was still clad in her white nightgown.

"Straight to the grave!" she said sincerely.

"Strange."

"What is that?"

"You have no flowers," he pointed out.

She stared at him blankly.

"Marina!"

They both turned as her name was called. Armand was hurrying toward her, a large bundle of wildflowers in his hands.

"I think you've forgotten these," he said, his expression entirely guileless. "Lord Baristo, we're ready; your party awaits."

Carlo looked from one of them to the other, seeking the conspiracy in Armand's timely appearance. They both returned his stare with complete innocence.

"Fine, then. I shall see you later, my lady. This evening, at supper."

"Yes," she said, and again started by. "I fear so," she muttered beneath her breath.

"What?" he demanded.

She stopped, and turned back. "I certainly hope so," she said sweetly.

"Marina," he replied slowly, "you are going now?" There was doubt and an edge to his tone.

"Yes, now, right now, of course."

"Your feet are bare," Carlo noted.

"In honor of my parents," she said quickly.

"Part of your vow, eh?"

"Oh, yes!" And smiling, she turned and started out—ruing the fact she had no shoes. Lendo was a place of incredible beauty, with cliffs and hills rising high from the sea, and within the great mass of rocks and rises, there were fields and forests, all offering a rich bounty. They were blessed with plentiful fishing, and an abundance of game in the forests, wild hogs, rabbits, pheasants, and more. But the walk up the cliffs and through the plateaus was not a pleasant one in bare feet. Still—this small torment was nothing compared to the torture of a day spent hunting with Carlo Baristo. Determined, she kept walking.

She had cleared the castle, built into a low level of cliffs, and was on the rise when she heard the sound of hoofbeats behind her. Turning, she saw that Armand had ridden out with her mare, Arabella. He dismounted quickly, giving her a hand up into the saddle. He winked as he did so. "You didn't mention anything about *not riding* in all those vows."

She smiled down at him. "Thank you, cousin."

"My pleasure, Marina." He bowed deeply. "I am off, then." He shrugged. "Who knows? Maybe Carlo, Count Baristo, will meet up with a killer rabbit. One can only hope!"

He turned back before she could reply. Both heartened and further depressed, Marina rode onward, very grateful to Armand.

She stopped at the site of her parents' graves, laid her flowers, and said her prayers. But then she moved on, to one of the cliffs, and toward a plateau where she often came. It was near the caves that were rumored to harbor the menacing Dragon in the Den. She didn't believe in the dragon, though there were lovely stories told about the way her father had rescued her mother. There was even an underlying superstition in the village that the dragon was as old as man, that he had come before, demanding a sacrifice each year, and if the strength and peace of Lendo ever began to fail, the dragon could come again.

She loved the area herself. There were places touched by beautiful foliage, streams and rivers, and delicate waterfalls. And there was the ancient area, a place where pillars stood, where carved stone seats remained, and it was possible to wonder about the people who created such a charming little realm of both tranquility and mystery.

Marina sat on one of the small benches and curled her feet beneath her. She was actually quite fond of being alone—it was a way to sit and imagine that there had been a dragon, and that it must have been spectacular, her father defying a mighty beast to save her mother. Yet even as she began to imagine the creature, she was aware she had company. Turning around, she saw her friend, the strange, self-proclaimed mystic, Radifini.

Her stepfather dismissed Radifini as a crazy old hermit; Radifini himself insisted he was a wizard, and that he had been a man of great esteem in days of old that were still not so long ago—and he could not believe so many had forgotten his powers!

Marina wasn't certain where he actually lived, except that it had to be here, somewhere in the cliffs. He told her that, indeed, his home—where he still looked hard to foresee the future and gaze over all that was left of Lendo and the house of d'Or—was within the cliffs. But he never asked her there, for it was dangerous sometimes to foresee the future.

As dangerous as it could be to scoff at a belief in dragons.

"So, my lady, you are here again," he said sternly. "Dreaming. What—they have no pots and pans for you to scrub today? The servants are all in attendance, and the Countess of Baristo has not warned your stepfather that you must make the beds or polish the silver, since you are in truth but an orphan now, and must be prepared to offer more than blue eyes and a pretty smile if you are to make a good match?"

"I'm here again," she said, "because apparently, they are all delighted, thinking they have found the finest match in the world for me."

"Oh?" Radifini joined her on the bench. "And who would this illustrious suitor be?"

"Carlo, Count of Baristo. It will be a Christmas wedding. Daphne will be married as well, to Michelo, son of the great Duke Fiorelli."

"Ah," Radifini said gravely. He patted her knee. "Well, then."

Marina sighed, leaning her elbows upon her knees. "Well, then," she repeated.

"Merry Christmas?" he offered weakly. She rewarded him with an angry glare.

"Ah, well. You're less than pleased," Radifini noted. "He's rich, powerful, handsome, some would say."

"I think that he's really a reptile," Marina told him.

"And you're running away—in bare feet, cloak, and nightgown?"

"I'm not running away," she said.

"So you've agreed to the marriage?"

"I've not said a word."

"And why not?"

"I can't leave Lendo. I must stay—it's bad enough that my stepfather rules, with the wretched Countess of Baristo always at his side! I think she has designs upon him. Her husband is gone, as is my mother. But d'Artois is not really so cruel, and when I insist upon the old traditions and holidays, he listens. So . . . I must stay. And make sure that I am in a position of power, as well."

"What if Baristo is a reptile, and makes you miserable?"

She laughed. "I'm probably quite capable of making him very miserable, as well."

"But that's no real life," Radifini said. He stroked his long white beard. "And not as it should be . . . Why, I remember when your parents were married; indeed, I remember when you were born! I was there, with all my power, and my white magic . . . and still, we lost them far too soon."

Marina placed a hand affectionately over his. "I am sure that you loved my parents, and that you were always there for them."

"Mock me if you will, young lady. The belief in magic is lost, so none of you young people seem to know what is out there, what glory, what danger. I did more than love your parents. I countered a great deal of evil, but . . . some are blind to what they can't see, touch, or feel, and they don't believe when they should. And always, if one looks, there's so much in the heart. But your father . . . perhaps he was too good a man. Still, you know. I serve the house of d'Or, and the day will come when I am able to make a difference!"

She squeezed his hand gently. "Radifini, you make a difference every time I see you! I love to listen to you. You bring back the real splendor of Lendo, and you give me back the laughter and spirit of my parents. You're a really wondrous white wizard, I do believe it!"

She thought that he was about to shake his head sadly, and insist she didn't really believe what couldn't be felt, seen, or touched, and their downfall might well be in that lack of vision. But just as they sat together, there was a disturbance in the brush. Jumping up, Marina first thought she saw an animal—a very large wolf? A horse?—coming low through the brush. But there was nothing. The sun made a sudden shift in the sky then, and a ray of light, almost dazzling, touched down upon the old pillars and seats of the small cove.

She blinked, certain she saw a woman slipping behind one of the pillars and into the ruins beyond. But the light had blinded her; she didn't know exactly what she had seen.

"Radifini, did you—"

"Sh!" he warned softly.

Then she heard the sound, as well. Horses coming, riding hard upon the plateau.

She wrapped her cloak around her and stood very still. In seconds, Carlo, Count of Baristo, came into the small clearing area, his huge mount pawing the earth and working its bit. He was joined by one of his huntsmen.

"Ah, Marina! Imagine . . . you've fulfilled your vow—and so quickly. No matter, you must leave. There's danger here. We've been hunting a wolf. It's wounded now . . . running. Have you seen the creature?"

"A wolf . . . wounded," she said. She turned and pointed far across the plateau, in a far distant direction. "Perhaps . . . I saw something. Low to the ground, running."

Carlo narrowed his eyes, then stared sharply at Radifini. "You—hermit! What did you see?"

"As my lady says, there was something, yes, low to the ground, running."

Carlo nodded, stared at Marina, then spoke to his companion. "Flush out the ruins. If Marina says one way, the beast has gone the other."

Both men turned their horses. On instinct, Marina ran after them. "Wait, no . . . !"

In a moment, she would hear their cries of pleasure as they went in for the kill . . . if what she had seen had been a wounded wolf, and the sun had teased her eyes and shown her a human form instead. She might hear the mournful cry of a creature, cornered . . . baying out its last gasp of breath . . . then meeting the steel death doled out by such a man as Carlo.

She caught up with Carlo, grabbed him by the leg, and stopped him as he sat on the saddle. "Don't be daft. I'd tell you if there was a maddened wolf nearby!"

As he looked down at her, there was a sudden disturbance from the bush. Something large moved through the foliage.

"A wild pony!" Marina murmured. "Nothing more, I'm certain." She looked at Carlo. "A harmless creature! If there is a wounded wolf, it has not come this way. Trust me on this, I beg of you—I'd not let others be harmed by a predator!"

"Go, ride after the dangerous beast, my lord!" Radifini said.

"Marina, you must come," Carlo said. "Ride with me. There is danger here."

"I will defend her," Radifini said.

"You, old man!" Carlo mocked. "You could not defend her from a fly."

"I'm quite capable of defending myself, thank you," Marina said. "And Carlo, I do believe you underestimate our friend Radifini."

"I tell you, young lord, there is no wolf here!" Radifini insisted.

"Marina, you should come."

"I am still in meditation."

"With the old man?"

"I remember her parents with deeper love than any," Radifini said solemnly.

"Be back by supper," Carlo said impatiently. "Or I shall fear for you, indeed, Marina, and come to insist that I keep my eye upon you, at all times."

He rode off, his huntsman following quickly after.

"Reptile!" Marina said with a sigh.

"Snake, perhaps," Radifini agreed. He wrinkled his nose. "Frog."

"Too noble. He's a toad!" she argued, managing to smile. But memory served her, and her smile faded. She kissed the old man's cheek. "I must go. I don't know what I saw, but brave Carlo was hunting down some poor wounded beast. I must see if I can find the creature. It might be injured. God knows—that *was* Carlo. He might truly have shot at a wild pony or horse, seeing a big, bad wolf in his mind's eye! I'm sorry, I don't mean to be rude to you, or leave you. I do enjoy our time together so much!"

"Good heavens, my girl! Go find the creature, and hurry now," he told her.

The sun had become warm. Marina dropped her cloak upon the rocks to move more quickly over the rough terrain, through the long grasses, trees, and foliage. Scampering along carefully, she followed the strange tracks she could barely discern upon the ground, thanking God all the while that Carlo had *not* been hunting with hounds.

She crawled through boulders and brush, swore softly as she stepped on stones. At last she broke out near the edge of a cliff, and there, upon the smooth surface of a weatherworn rock, belly down, struggling for comfort, was the creature.

Not a pony, or a wolf, or any animal that ran upon all fours. It was a falcon. A magnificent falcon!

"Poor creature!" she said softly. Blood poured from the animal's wing. A broken arrow shaft protruded from it and she cried out softly, hoping the arrow itself had not imbedded into any bone, breaking the wing.

"Easy!" she murmured, aware she could be severely injured by the beak of the bird should she frighten it. As gently as she could, she touched the creature, carefully feeling the point of the arrow tip. "Poor, poor thing!" she murmured. It seemed only the tip of the arrow had made it into the wing, and that the wound was not too deep. Placing her hand hard at the point of impact to staunch any flow of blood, she gripped the arrow tip. "It will hurt, I'm afraid," she said softly. "I hope you can realize that I'm trying to help you! Be easy, now . . . it definitely is going to hurt a bit."

Carefully, she grasped the bird, set pressure to the wound, and pulled out the arrow.

"A bit!" came a shout. "A bit! That hurt like blue blazes!"

Marina was so startled by the voice she nearly fell off the rocky plateau where she had found the creature. She had been seated; she leapt to her feet, looking around, searching out the surrounding foliage.

There was no one. No one near . . .

She looked back at the falcon.

"Yes, you silly girl, it's me speaking!" came the voice again. "Me, here, the falcon."

Incredulous, Marina walked back toward the injured animal.

"Me, here, yes!"

The beak was moving. The falcon definitely appeared to be . . . *speaking*.

"I'm losing my mind," Marina murmured. "Stress . . . has to be stress. Surely—and certainly, not surprising—the very idea of marrying the Count Baristo could cause madness."

"Stress . . . overload . . . there's every excuse in the world!" the falcon sighed.

"Falcons don't talk!" Marina said.

"Have you ever actually addressed one and *expected* an answer from it?"

"Well, no . . ."

"Then how on earth would you know that we don't talk? I would say that, apparently, sometimes we do!" the falcon said irritably. "Now, please, have you forgotten all about me? My injury? Have you something to use as a bandage? Come, come, girl! Catch your jaw before it hits the dirt. Get over here and help!"

Chapter 2

With a great, heavy blow that extended every ounce of his strength, Michelo, heir apparent to the great Duke Fiorelli, brought his battle sword down upon the shoulders of his opponent. He had done so already, time and time again, and each time, the mail- and armor-clad being had risen again, like some monster, able to turn on him once more with renewed strength.

He heard the great clash of steel against steel; he felt the reverberation sweep through his arm, and then the length of him.

And then . . . thank God! The man . . . the *thing* stayed down. Michelo drew in a deep breath, anxious to approach his fallen enemy and pull the visor and helmet from the face. The warriors of old insisted they had fought wartrolls, mercenary creatures brought in by their enemies, beings that had scales rather than flesh. He'd never seen one, and he'd wondered at times if the wartroll hadn't been invented by strong men, unwilling to admit they could not face an enemy with an even greater strength. And yet, in the time of his father's days of battle, they had beat back such an army, won a decisive victory. And over the many years since, there had been comparative peace . . . with just a few raids now and then.

But their enemies grew bolder, encroaching upon lands where the people lived in freedom from barbarous rules and overbearing tyrants. There is strength in alliance, his father had taught him, and so it had been true. But now . . .

The legendary Nico d'Oro was gone. Carlo Baristo swore he would raise his army, and come to aid at the border when a real threat existed. Only Michelo's own father believed the raids were coming far more often now, and with far greater intensity. And so, Michelo had now spent most of the past few years on the border, leading his men against the raiders, and wondering when the time would come when the enemy rose en masse, assaulting them in greater numbers. They would override his father's lands first, and if the duchy fell, the counties of Lendo and Baristo would not be far behind.

Michelo shook his head with aggravation. The alliance of the duchy and the two counties had now been formed for years and years, but one would think, sometimes, that Baristo was not much of an ally to have—sometimes it seemed as if he worked against the very peace they fought so hard along the borders to maintain.

He moved toward his enemy. Just then, though, he heard the hoofbeats that signaled the coming of his own men, who, in riding against the enemy, had come to assist. They had been in hand-to-hand battles themselves, and only now were rallying again to regroup behind him.

He turned to see them riding quickly, eager to come to his aid and defense should he have been caught off-guard by more opponents.

He waved, then turned back, so anxious to lift that helmet and see if he had battled a man—or the rumored beast-enemy of his father's day.

The grass was empty. There was nothing there. No man, and certainly, no beast.

He knelt down as his men rode hard behind him. Antonio Tosse from the north jumped from his horse, landing at his side.

"He escaped?" he said.

"He was down . . . and now he's gone . . . so he must have. But surely you saw him rise and run," Michelo said.

"We saw nothing," Antonio said.

Michelo touched a dark spot on the earth, and studied the tip of the finger of his gauntlet. Blood. There had been someone, something . . . wounded. And now it was gone. "Search for a trail," he said.

And so they searched, and there were scatters of blood, and yet no trail.

"What manner of man . . . ?" Michelo murmured.

"Wartroll," Antonio said.

"Wartroll . . . a race we know little about, yet it seems indeed our enemies fight with some magic. They come in hordes . . . they are gone as if they were never there," offered Andreas Este, a man who had been a farmer, and honed his skills through many years to become a warrior.

The sound of hoofbeats came to them.

Antonio stood. "There's a rider coming. Carrying your father's banner."

As they waited, the lone rider, heralding the banner of the Duke of Fiorelli, came hard among them. He dismounted quickly, bowing to them all, and handed Michelo a letter, sealed in wax with his father's great signet ring.

They all waited as Michelo opened the letter, read the words, and stared at them again.

"I am summoned home," he said.

"But . . ." Antonio said. He fell silent. They all knew what his words would be. *But they remained in danger. Riders came, warriors attacked. Their forces on the front were few, and in the time he had spent here, the men had come to follow him.*

"I will not be gone long," he said quietly. "It seems my father has decided I must marry. A great ceremony, at Christmas. There are more than our forces at risk, so it seems. He believes that I have gone quite far enough alone, and in leading you all against the risk of invasion, I risk leaving the duchy with no heir."

"Ah," Antonio said.

"Um," Andreas murmured.

"Your father has found you this bride?" Antonio said.

"There's nothing at all unusual in that," Andrea reminded him.

"But parents find brides for their sons in order to cement alliances, to form treaties, to gain land," Antonio said sadly.

"She could be five hundred pounds," Andreas mused.

"Or an old hag," Antonio suggested.

"Or have a mustache, a unibrow!" Andreas added with horror.

"A true witch!" the messenger said, unable to refrain. They all looked at him. "Sorry, Lord Michelo.

It's been known to happen."

"I know of my intended bride," Michelo said. "Daphne, the daughter of the new Lord of Lendo, Count d'Artois." Count d'Artois had ruled Lendo for many years by that time, but he was still known as the "new" Lord of Lendo.

"Then she's not hideous," Antonio said.

"Or huge, six feet by six feet," Andreas agreed.

"Or even a terrible witch," the messenger added.

"No, she is none of those," Michelo said, folding the letter. "In my absence, you will all follow the command of Antonio, and I swear I will not leave you long. You, my friend," he told the messenger, "ride back quickly now, and tell my father I am coming, as soon as I make a few preparations—as in bathing," he added ruefully.

The messenger mounted his horse, and turned back the way he had come.

"You don't look like a joyous bridegroom," Antonio remarked.

"Or even terribly relieved that you're not to marry a six-by-six old crone of a witch!" Andreas added.

"With a mustache," Antonio added.

"Or a unibrow," Andreas added.

"I am relieved," Michelo said, smiling ruefully.

"You're just not happy," Antonio said.

"How observant!" Andreas quipped. Antonio furled his brow, and stared at Andreas.

Michelo laughed. "No, I'm not happy."

"But . . . Daphne is quite lovely," Antonio said.

"I saw her years ago, yes. And those who speak of her do so glowingly. I just hadn't thought . . . well, I don't love her at all. And she can hardly care for me. She hasn't seen me. I mean . . . it's not what I thought, in my heart, I suppose, when I did think of marriage, and the future."

"I'm afraid that *I* would take the six-by-six, wrinkled, pruned, mustached, old hag—to improve my holdings," Antonio told him cheerfully. "Good heavens, man! You're getting married. What has that to

do with love?"

"Nothing, so it seems," Michelo said, dusting his gauntlets against his thigh, then heading toward the horses. His own great warhorse, Alexander, named for the powerful Greek conqueror, awaited him. They would be truly allying the lands of the duchy, and those of Lendo. And there was no argument with his father's logic. The great duke had it all figured out; Michelo would marry Daphne, and apparently Carlo, Count of Barristo, would marry the other daughter of the house.

He couldn't help but think of Carlo with a certain weary displeasure.

But then . . .

At least the man wasn't being married to Adriana, his own younger sister!

So. It was all carefully planned. It was logical. It spun ties between everyone in the duchy, right and proper.

It was just . . .

Just what?

There had to be more.

Aye, it seemed . . .

There just had to be more!

Marina staunched the flow of blood from the falcon's wing. "Let's see if the bleeding begins again," she murmured, resting the creature back on the rock.

"You're not leaving me without this bandaged properly, are you?" the creature demanded.

Marina smiled. "No . . . I just want to make sure you're not going to bleed to death in the imminent future! We may need more pressure for a few minutes. It's a miracle a bone wasn't broken. That your body wasn't . . . well, that it wasn't more serious."

The flow of blood staunched, Marina sat back, assuring herself that the bleeding would not begin

again. Weary then, Marina rested her head against the rock as well for a moment, wishing that she could stay, and sleep, and then wake, and find her world had changed.

This was it, apparently. Life had become too much for her. She had assumed she could manage whatever came, that she was strong and determined, and would never leave Lendo completely in the hands of such a man as Carlo Baristo.

But now she knew. She wasn't that strong. She was losing her mind. Hearing words come from a falcon. Perhaps it was a good thing she should lose her mind. Carlo wouldn't want to marry a lunatic. Ah, but then again! He might marry her, and have her locked up. Carlo coveted Lendo, and marrying her would eventually bring him the land. Her stepfather coveted his social standing more than property, and thus Daphne would marry Fiorelli's son.

She needed to fight this, because insanity wasn't going to save her.

"You know, I'm not really a falcon," the bird said.

Smiling, Marina lifted her head. "You look like a falcon." She was somewhat amused, still not certain she was in her own right mind.

"How many times have you seen animals talk?"

"Never, we've established that. But animals do, in their way, talk all the time. We usually just have to listen differently."

The falcon sighed with feigned patience. "How many talk, as I am talking now?"

"None, but I don't believe you're really talking."

"What?"

"This is a figment of my imagination. I'm choosing a dream world over the travesty of my reality."

For a moment the falcon was silent, dark eyes hard upon her. *"What?"*

"I'm dreaming this whole thing up."

"Snap out of it, young woman!" the falcon said impatiently. "My dear child, if your life is that distressing, I may be able to help you. If I can actually get your full attention," the bird said with another sigh, this one very openly *im*patient. "My name is Thomasina. And I'm really a rather talented fairy."

"Oh?" Marina smiled. "Of course." She peered closely at the animal's wing again. "I just want to see that wound. I think the bleeding has stopped completely." With fabric torn from her nightgown, Marina began to bandage the falcon's wing. "So—if you're really a fairy, why do you appear to be a falcon with an arrow wound on your wing?"

"Well, you see, I was actually doing a bit of eavesdropping earlier today," Thomasina, the falcon, said. "Ouch!"

"I'm securing the bandaging as carefully as I can. It would be much easier, of course, if you really were a fairy, if you'd pop back to a human-like form. An arm would be far easier to tend to than a wing, you know."

"Fairies, you know, can shift shapes quite easily," Thomasina said.

"Then it would be so convenient and helpful if you were to shift now."

"You're not letting me finish the story. I had to get away quickly—there are those who should never be given a chance to catch a fairy—and so I turned myself into a wolf. Bad choice, I'm afraid, made too quickly. Then the monster who put the arrow into me was on my tail, and that time, just a bit belatedly, I thought *falcon*. But now, you see . . . I'm quite weakened by all this, so I must remain in this form."

"As you say."

"Young lady, you are quite patronizing."

"I don't mean to be."

"Oh, that's right. You believe yourself to be in the midst of a serious mind disease."

"What I think is that I'm going to see you're well bandaged and set for the night. Then I'm heading home, and I'll soak in a long bath, and"—she paused, making a face—"I'll go to supper, as I must, of course, drink a great quantity of wine to get through it, and sleep just as long as I possibly can. You mustn't worry, though. I will be back tomorrow."

"You can't tell anyone that I'm a magical being."

"I hadn't intended to in the least."

The falcon stared at her, angling its head. "What are you doing up here in your nightdress?"

Marina laughed. "Hm, quickly—I'm supposed to marry this awful man I despise. But I'm going to do so, because I think it's really the right thing. I don't like being home because my parents are gone, my stepfather is a wishy-washy man led around by a woman who is a witch, and it's rather miserable. That's about it. I come here to . . . dream, I guess," she said softly.

"And that's why you wear your nightgown? The better to dream?"

Marina shook her head, smiling. "The better to escape quickly—I had to pretend I was heading out, rather than be forced to join a hunting party. I have a cloak, somewhere, and my horse is not far away."

"You do seem to be having a strange existence. As I said, I can help you. Fairies can grant a human three wishes, you know. At Christmastide. It's quite convenient for you that it happens to be Christmastide."

"Ah, Thomasina, what a sweet thought! But I do believe that we must help ourselves in life. I could run away, you see, but I don't think that would do anyone any good. I love Lendo very much, and I do think I'm quite a match for the wretched fellow I'm to marry."

"Well . . ." the falcon said softly. "I am, of course, pleased to hear you have confidence in yourself, but . . . well, my dear, even the strongest man, or the most powerful lord, needs assistance at some point in life."

"True, but I will be just fine. Of course . . . if there were any other way . . . but there isn't. So."

"So. Your life is wretched—but you're resigned. And so you come here . . . and spend your days in dreams. I'm not so sure that's helping you. Three wishes, girl. Take a chance."

Marina laughed. "Well, I must say, I'd enjoy it heartily if that swaggering braggart, Carlo Baristo, were to fall flat into a watering trough," she said, savoring the image her words brought to mind. Then she noted how far the sun had gone down, and she rose quickly. "I must go. I believe you're fairly sheltered here . . . and close enough to the water to drink. I'll be back as soon as I can in the morning to make sure you're doing well. I wish you a good night and a speedy recovery. And I still can't believe I'm talking to a falcon. Or rather, that a falcon is talking to me!"

"I've told you, I'm not really a falcon, I'm a fairy, a good one, named Thomasina."

Marina grinned. "Well, you know the old saying, if it looks like a falcon, talks like a falcon, and so forth. You are a beautiful creature! And whatever you are, don't worry, I swear I will see you completely healed! But now I must run!"

She blew the bird a kiss, and hurried back the way she had come, collecting the cloak she had doffed earlier and whistling for her mare. Luckily, the horse had not wandered far, and Marina started back far ahead of the coming dusk.

She reached the courtyard, however, to find the hunting party had returned before she did. The men had dismounted, and several were still speaking as their horses slaked their thirst at the watering trough. Hoping she still might not run into Carlo, she rode Arabella through to the stables, and there, dismounted quickly, softly calling her cousin's name.

"Armand?"

"Armand is busy."

Carlo stepped from the stall where his huge charger was kept. "Just returning? You're dedicated to your mourning. I hope you find such zeal for other pursuits, as well."

She ignored his words.

"Were you able to kill the wolf?" she asked politely.

"We never found the wolf."

"Oh, well, I'm sure you gravely injured the beast."

"Did you find the wolf, Marina?"

"No."

"Are you lying?"

She laughed. "I can swear by all the saints, I saw no wolf after you departed to chase such a beast!" She wondered what he would say if she told him she'd spent the latter part of the day tending to the wound of a falcon—that talked.

"You would try," he said, "to heal a wolf, no matter how dangerous. Indeed, it seems you are determined to save any bedraggled creature."

"I'm sorry, I'm lost—to what 'creature' do you refer now?"

"That crazy old hermit."

She leaned against Arabella, a slow smile curving her lips. "Radifini? He is a friend."

"Quite insane, I believe."

"Oh, I don't think so. He claims to have been a great wizard, in my father's day."

"Rubbish!" Carlo said, and nearly spit out the words. "Great wizard?"

"Well, if not, then he is a harmless old man. And a friend."

He started toward her. "You'll have to learn that there isn't really enough time in the day to spend so many hours with old madmen who have delusions of grandeur."

"The old madman was dear to my parents, and I'll not forget him."

He was coming too close; she moved to the other side of Arabella, hoping he wouldn't pen her in the animal's stall as she removed her mare's saddle and bridle.

For the second time that day, Armand came to the rescue, striding into the stables. "Marina, you're back. I'll see to Arabella for you, since your stepfather expects you to join the company at supper."

"Thank you, Armand." He took the reins, winking. She mouthed, "Bless you." She wanted to say so much more to him! Even if he didn't believe she'd rescued a talking falcon that claimed to be a fairy, he'd laugh with her about her escape into a fantasy world.

But not now. Now was the time to escape.

She strode quickly across the stables, and winced when she heard the footsteps following in her wake.

"Marina!"

She pretended not to hear.

"Marina!"

She had reached the watering trough, and there were still too many men and horses surrounding it. She paused, turning.

He came to her and took her hand. "Your stepfather and my mother intend to discuss the wedding plans tonight. It will be something of a celebration. We'll drink to one another this evening, my dear."

She managed not to wrench her hand away; far too many of his men were looking on.

"Drinking tonight sounds good," she said sweetly.

She turned again. She had no idea he meant to hold on to her. She walked into the neck of one of the horses, ducked, and kept going. At that point, she realized he had not let go.

Nor did he intend to do so.

She tried to duck back beneath the neck of the horse, but the animal chose that moment to move as well, turning its body in a sudden swing.

Carlo's grip on her was firm—he had apparently meant to prove he didn't have to let her go, that she was dismissed only when he chose.

If he'd only let her go . . .

But he didn't, and so the great warhorse turned sideways into him, and he was swept off his feet . . .

And into the watering trough.

He fell backward, flat out, and went under, and it was one of the funniest things she had ever seen in her life. His hands and feet were waving above the surface until his head broke the waterline, as well.

He was bright red, spouting water through his lips as if he were a fountain.

His men laughed.

She couldn't help it; she burst into laughter, as well.

And then, as quickly as it had begun, all the laughter ended, for Carlo Baristo stared at all of them with eyes so furious they seemed to glow. Manolo, his squire, so often at his side, let out a laugh when all had gone silent. Carlo's head turned with the speed of a cobra, and his furious gaze settled upon Manolo, who then pretended to hiccup, and went silent.

"Get me out of here!" he raged furiously.

His men sprang forward.

It would have been a fine time to make a retreat, but Marina was still savoring the sight of him, soaked and bedraggled.

He was pulled from the water, and gave no thanks to those who were soaked from their efforts to help him. He marched over to Marina, shaking with a fury that startled her. His voice was a rush of air that

held so much malice, she felt chilled to the bone.

"You did that on purpose," he hissed.

Stunned, she arched a brow. "I didn't do that at all. You are such a gallant man, who'd have imagined that you'd have such a hold on me when I turned away? And you can't blame a horse for behaving like one!"

"I will have the animal slain, Marina, and then, perhaps, you'll understand how I feel about being viciously humiliated."

"Slain!" she cried. "Not even you are so cruel or careless with life!"

"I warn you, I will do so."

She spoke loudly suddenly, staring at him with eyes that belied every word out of her mouth. "Thank God, my dear Count Baristo, that you are so magnanimous a man, that your temper is so quickly brought to good humor! Truly, forgive me that you are soaked to the bone, and I pray you're not too chilled. That was entirely my fault, my absolute lack of grace. I pray, please forgive *me* for causing your mishap, but then again . . . dear sir! Why, indeed, you are soaked, and yet . . . so manly for it all! Your muscles, sir, bulge right through the dampness of the cloth. Wet, my lord, you are indeed something to behold!"

She smiled icily. "I think all your men heard that. Does the horse live?"

"The *horse* will live," he said pleasantly.

"Is that a threat against my life?" she demanded.

"Against the daughter of the great d'Or? Never . . . or at least, not, my lady, in the foreseeable future." He bowed, doffing his drenched hat. Water, of course, sprayed all over her, spattering her cloak.

She didn't mind at all. "At supper then," he said, "we drink to the future."

"Oh, yes, we'll drink!"

She turned and retreated quickly up the stairs to her room in the rear of the castle. And it wasn't until she was there that she remembered talking to the falcon, and the words that she had said herself—wish number one.

"Well, I must say, I'd enjoy it heartily if that swaggering braggart, Carlo Baristo, were to fall flat into a watering trough!"

And he had done so.

Carlo had fallen into a watering trough!

Well, Carlo was certain she had pushed him into a watering trough!

And he had threatened to kill a horse for the act!

But still . . .

She smiled. It had been miraculously funny while it had gone on. She couldn't remember when she had laughed so, and she didn't even mind when he thought he had forced her to apologize. He never realized he was being mocked for he assumed he was so fine a specimen that surely she meant her every word sincerely.

Marina threw herself upon her bed and stared at the ceiling. If she wasn't losing her mind, the falcon had been talking. And claiming to be a fairy . . .

A fairy who had offered her three wishes at Christmastide!

She had wanted Carlo to fall into a watering trough. She had made the wish, and perhaps, thus, she *had* been the one to make it happen.

There was a tapping on her door. The caller did not wait for a reply to bid enter. The wooden door was pushed open.

Geovana was there. Tall, with perfect posture, she seemed able to glide with squared and regal shoulders as she walked. Thin-faced, frightening, yet elegant, she had come to a point in life where she was always in perfect composure, where her voice was always even, where only the slight glint of golden evil in her eyes might give a clue to the fact her machinations were in any way to improve her own lot. She wore black most of the time, in memory, of course, of those departed. Yet her sleek gowns were edged with royal blues and silver, touches of color that spoke of her nobility. When Elisia had married Pietro, Geovana had actually worn white to the wedding. Ah, but now, Elisia was gone, and Geovana had all but taken over the castle at Lendo; Count d'Artois seemed to give the gravest attention to her every word, as if he were hypnotized by the very sound of her voice.

"Good evening . . . my dear. The finest wine is being served below, in your honor. And that of my dear son, of course. He'll be joining us shortly . . . as it seems you played a naughty little prank on him."

She might have been the most magnanimous woman in the world. She seemed so remote, and yet . . . such a touch of kindly doting!

Marina rose quickly.

"I will be right there, Countess Baristo. I need but a minute to myself."

"Dear child, of course." The Countess walked on into the room, pausing before Marina. She set a hand upon her cheek, and kissed her forehead.

Marina felt an arctic chill sweep over her.

"What a lovely daughter-in-law you'll be!" she said, and then turned, moving with an eerie silence. Geovanna departed, closing the door behind her.

If only the falcon did really talk . . .

And if only Marina did have three wishes. Three Christmas wishes.

But then . . .

It was true. Absolutely true that the Count Baristo *had* just fallen into a watering trough.

Just exactly as she had *wished*.

If so, one wish used . . .

Two were left.

Chapter 3

M ichelo Fiorelli rode out by night.

There was a full moon shining overhead, and Alexander knew the way as well as he did himself. This side of the border, peace had reigned for years, and so he rode with little thought given to distance or direction, nearly dozing at times.

He was loathe to leave the battlefield, afraid there was a greater power behind the enemy attacks than had been shown thus far. He remained disturbed by the way the body of the warrior who had so viciously fought had simply vanished, not seen by either him or his men.

Touched by moonlight, the landscape was beautiful. Sloping hills to the sea appeared to be blanketed in dark mauve. Here and there, cliffs caught a reflection of moonlight, and glowed in a softened beauty. He loved his homeland. Loved it intensely. He had been willing to fight and die for it now for many years, and had been ever vigilant.

And it made sense . . .

Though there was now the lovely young Adriana to fill his father's days with happiness, Michelo was the great duke's only son. It was natural his father wanted a continuation of his line.

And still . . .

If he recalled the last time he'd seen Daphne, she had been a lovely girl. They'd both been courteous and polite. And he'd felt . . .

Nothing.

And she, in return, had appeared to make the proper moves, to be courteous and attentive when he spoke. And yet, she had looked at him with as much enthusiasm as . . .

A piece of wilted lettuce.

"Whoa!" he murmured suddenly, startled into awareness as Alexander stumbled on the path. Just then, clouds slipped over the moon, and darkness fell like an encompassing blanket over the land. At the same time, almost exactly, so it seemed, a fog swept in from the sea.

Alexander snorted and whinnied.

Michelo patted his horse's neck. "It's all right, old boy. We'll go just ahead, there are caves down the path to the sea. We'll stop there, and make it home by tomorrow."

Alexander tossed his head, as if understanding perfectly. Then suddenly, in the darkness, he reared up, snorting with panic.

Michelo was nearly unhorsed, but held his ground. Out of the swirling darkness, he saw cloaked men had used the cover of darkness to move stealthily upon them. He drew his sword from the sheath in his saddle, then cried out to Alexander. The horse reared up again, then plunged forward. As the first of the men came forward, a flicker in the darkness showed the length of his sword. Michelo swung against his enemy, catching the figure with the impetus of Alexander's forward motion.

One hung on his left, and one on his right. One had a knife, and planned to use it against the horse to slow him down. He struck that figure with his sword hilt; in silence it fell away. The other clung to his saddle and leg, tearing at him with superhuman strength. Michelo brought the blade of his sword down twice . . . three times . . .

At last the figure fell away.

They raced onward, Michelo trying to slow his horse's gait, for they raced into a stygian darkness. He and Alexander were rising again, climbing to the cliffs.

"Whoa, boy, it's over! We're safe!" he cried, and a smile slipped onto his lips as he congratulated himself with great relief upon escaping the danger. "Safe!"

But even as he spoke, Alexander walked beneath an unseen tree.

A large, low branch caught Michelo squarely in the forehead.

With a slight groan, he fell from the horse, and the darkness of the night was complete.

Even with the great Duke Fiorelli, his lovely wife, Lucia, and their pretty young Adriana in attendance, Geovana took her seat at the side of Pietro d'Artois, Count of Lendo, for the evening's festivities.

"One would think she was countess here," Armand murmured to Marina, passing her on his way to the rear of the room, a far table, where falconers were allowed to sit. Marina grimaced, for it was true. The chair Geovana took had been her mother's seat, a place of honor. But then again, she was a countess in her own right, and it was her son's marriage that would be announced that night to the stepdaughter of the house, just as the marriage of Michelo, son of the great Fiorelli, would be announced, to Count d'Artois's beloved child of his blood, Daphne.

Marina didn't particularly care where anyone sat. All she wanted was for the night to be over.

At Geovana's departure from her bedroom, she had bathed and dressed correctly, or, at least, as correctly as she could, for the clothing that came her way tended to be the hand-me-downs from Daphne. She wondered that night if she lied to herself; if she didn't resent the fact that Daphne had come into her home, and been the one to receive the lessons, the love, the clothing, the doting of the older generation. Watching Daphne, she felt no real anger. Daphne was a beautiful young woman with a sweet disposition. She seemed a bit distracted, despite the fact she was tutored and adored—while Marina was given the chores. She didn't seem to be a terrible person, to ever cause ill to others. Since Marina did not want the dictatorial attention of her stepfather, she was glad to take a step behind Daphne, she realized.

Unfortunately, tonight, they were about to share a fate, for Duke Fiorelli, Lucia, and Adriana were seated at the head table next to Pietro d'Artois and Geovana, who were laughing and happy and quite pleased. Serafina, Daphne's main tutor in the arts of dance and music, was at the table as well, sweet, and lovely, and though usually entirely serene, she looked slightly ill.

Marina, late, hurrying to her seat, saw that Daphne looked wan and pale, and not at all happy. She was seated next to the messenger standing in for Michelo Fiorelli, who had apparently not made it back yet

from his battles at the borders.

As Marina approached the table, the men stood. Carlo took her hand, looking for all the world like the courteous, handsome young lord, and she was greeted with affection by all. She offered Carlo an apology for her tardiness, and he gave her a smile and an assurance. "Soon, dear Marina, I assure you, you will learn manners, and never have to apologize again."

She didn't have a chance to reply. The great Duke Fiorelli rose, and the company fell silent. He announced first the engagement of Daphne to his son, Michelo, and then the engagement of Carlo Baristo and Marina, the daughter of the late, lamented Nico and Elisia. There was cheering around the hall, and then people were up, standing, kissing one another, and it seemed the whole hall rejoiced.

Marina saw Daphne's face, and she was startled to see her stepsister looked stricken. After a word with her father-in-law-to-be, she suddenly fled the hall. Puzzled, Marina watched her go. And when Carlo told her they would dance, Daphne's exit gave her courage. "Forgive me! There seems to be an ague about! Daphne has retired . . . I fear the same symptoms!"

Carlo hated illness. He doubted her, she knew.

He also hated to be around anyone ill.

She took advantage of his hesitance and fled.

That night, even as she went to bed, she heard the beat of horse's hooves below, and looked out the window. She felt a great and terrible sorrow, for there was her cousin, Armand, still tilting with scarecrows, more feverishly now, as any chance of his winning Daphne was waning.

The weddings had been set for a fortnight's time.

Christmas Day.

She woke just as the sun crept over the gorgeous heights and cliffs and bluffs of their region. And before anyone could stop her, she dressed, raced to the stables, saddled Arabella, and took off for the hills, praying all the while that the falcon was faring well.

Indeed, she seemed much better. She appeared to have walked to the water, and was graciously dipping her beak for a long cool drink. All in all, she was making a remarkable recovery.

"You look wonderful," Marina said softly, checking the bandaged site on the falcon's wing. There was no hint of renewed bleeding. "It's quite amazing. You'll be good as new quite soon."

"I do hope!" the falcon said, and stared at her with head angled in a birdlike way. "So, how was your evening, Marina?"

"Remarkable, as well," Marina said. Her lips twitched into a smile. "Well, disastrous, of course, as our marriages were announced. But, Thomasina! Before that, it was priceless! Carlo fell into a water trough. Of course, he says that I pushed him, but it was all his fault, I swear it. And, oh, when he went in, I laughed so hard. And his men laughed . . . until he gave us all the evil eye! Ah, but still . . . those moments were worth his wrath! Isn't that truly astounding, after our conversation yesterday?"

The falcon stared at her for a moment. She could have sworn that the animal was frowning. "Astounding? Let me see, dear, what part about my having the power to grant three wishes did you just not get? And, of course, I'm quite glad you enjoyed the spectacle of the man in the water, but since his dousing doesn't really change life for you any . . . it's my opinion that you think long and hard about your second wish!"

Marina returned Thomasina's stare. It was so difficult to believe in magic, in wishes. And yet, it had been just as the falcon had said.

Of course, it was difficult to believe in a falcon, and a talking falcon at that, especially one with a name like Thomasina!

But, then, of course, the falcon claimed to be a fairy.

"Could this be real?" she whispered.

"In life, child, we must always help ourselves. But can this be real? A talking falcon? Magic? Maybe magic is also what we make of it. If you stop and let it be, Christmas can be a time of magic. You see, young lady, magic can be in the soul, and come to different people in different ways. Here, my dear, think of the magic in your heart at Christmas." She ruffled and fixed her feathers. "Dear, dear. So much for my speeches—you must not waste another wish. Think long and hard, and tell me your heart's desire."

Marina arched a brow. "I can't make my heart's desire a wish, since what I want more than anything else in the world is *not* to marry Carlo, Count Baristo! In that, I might well lose Lendo, and it was where my parents lived and ruled and I was born, and where I really am needed."

"At least you're taking this seriously, and thinking carefully," the falcon said, seeming a bit relieved.

"So . . ." Marina mused, rising and pacing several steps around the falcon, still thinking that the creature might disappear at any moment, and she would discover the entire adventure was actually in her desperate imagination. "My heart's desire—" She stopped suddenly, turning to face the falcon. "One night," she said softly.

"One night?"

Marina nodded, smiling. "Just one night . . . with the man of my dreams. Someone who is as enchanted with *me* as Armand is with his Daphne. Someone who looks at me that way, who sees only my eyes, hears my voice . . . someone gallant, brave, strong, truly noble—not in title, but in deed, in thought . . . in care."

"That's all?" the falcon queried.

"Did I ask too much?"

"No, no, just checking. It's always good to state a wish clearly and precisely. This is a bit more complicated than a dunking in a watering trough. Go on, please."

"Well, of course, it would be great if he were also incredibly handsome, witty, and charming," Marina said with a grin and a shrug.

"It's your wish," the falcon told her.

"That's it, then," Marina said. "That's it—because I have decided my future is the one I must live, and as I told Armand—my cousin—I am determined if Carlo tries to make me miserable, I simply will not let him." She looked away. "I know how to battle him," she murmured. "So . . . what night shall it be?" she asked teasingly. "We are going to have to hurry here, you know."

"There's someone coming," the falcon said, her head cocked at an angle.

"Someone coming?" Marina spun around, anxious to put distance between herself and the falcon, lest it be Carlo, and he decide for some reason he needed to dispose of the magical creature.

To her surprise, she saw Armand on the hill, leading his horse and patting Arabella.

"Armand?"

He started at the sound of her voice and swung around quickly. Seeing her, he let out a sigh of relief.

"What are you doing here?"

"I was worried about you. After the excitement in the hall last night . . . you didn't appear in the least happy."

"I certainly wasn't in the least happy," she agreed, and smiled at him wistfully. "But, Armand, did you notice? Daphne looked absolutely . . . ashen! She isn't happy, either."

"Do you think she even knows that I exist?" Armand asked. He shook his head then, looking down. "I spend my days tilting with straw mannequins, praying . . ."

Since Marina still wasn't entirely convinced that she wasn't totally delusional herself, she'd worried about mentioning the falcon to anyone. But Armand was her cousin, and her dearest friend. "Armand . . . come with me."

He followed her back to the rock plateau, where the falcon stood, watching him warily.

Armand looked at Marina. "It's a falcon!" he said.

"Yes, I know. Her wing was wounded."

"A beautiful falcon!" he mused. "Poor thing! Injured. I'll have a look."

"She was struck by an arrow," Marina murmured.

"Carlo!" he exclaimed angrily.

He strode to the falcon, gently moving the bandage, tenderly touching the wing by the wound. He looked up. "Fine work," he told Marina.

"She can talk," Marina said.

"Indeed, I often think they communicate, falcons are such fine and intelligent animals," Armand said.

"No, I mean, seriously, she can talk."

"Certain cries and calls can mimic words, I suppose," Armand said, striving to be patient and understanding, since they were all under so much stress.

Marina sighed. "Thomasina, talk to him, please."

The falcon angled her head, staring at her, then at Armand.

"He's my cousin; it's all right!" Marina insisted.

"Be still!" Armand murmured suddenly, and he, too, cocked his head at an angle, rather like the falcon's. "There's someone else . . . nearby," he said.

Marina moved protectively to the falcon's side.

"It's all right," Armand told her. "If it's Carlo, I'll lead him away, somehow." He hesitated. "You can go on, care for your falcon . . . talk to it."

Armand, ever her champion, hurried away to help her in whatever way he might.

Daphne didn't like to admit to it, in any way, but she knew that she was jealous.

Oh, she was the apple of her father's eye, all right! And so . . . day after day, every day, there was something.

And usually something wretched.

Math lessons with the tedious Baldini.

Art with Signora Tuscanianni.

There was the class in which she had to spend hours walking across a room with a book on her head, and needlepoint, and dance, and music . . .

Well, the dance and music were not so horrible. Serafina was wonderful; she was Daphne's one insight into the world around their own lands, for Serafina had traveled and entertained great kings and queens across the world. Daphne had often thought that Serafina was secretly in love with her father, Pietro, but if so, Serafina kept her own council. Once, Serafina had told her that Pietro certainly seemed to be intrigued by—if not entirely in love with—Geovana.

"Only because she casts spells!" Daphne had assured her.

Yet, despite her affection for her tutor, Daphne resented the endless hours she was forced to give over to the proper classes. She knew that Serafina herself was puzzled that Marina—destined to marry Carlo—was not forced into the same endless round of learning. "It's most odd!" Serafina had said, "when she is to be Carlo's countess, unless . . ."

"Unless what?" Daphne had queried.

"No, no, that would be . . . far too horrid," Serafina had murmured, and would say no more.

So Daphne continued to envy Armand and her stepsister, Marina.

They were always free. Well, there were always numerous chores for them, but they both seemed to take that in stride. Day after day, she watched as they did their work, and disappeared. And sometimes, she would come upon Armand as he sat at a garden bench writing, and he would flush, and hide his poems, except for every so often when he would read one to her, and she would look into his eyes and marvel at the words, and the way he looked at her, at just the sound of his voice . . .

Then, someone would call her back to a class, remind her she was intended to be the wife of the son of the Great Duke Fiorelli, and Armand would be gone. Oh, yes, she was the child of privilege. And she envied the stepsister who was asked to see to the table settings, the linens, and even, sometimes, the ashes in the hearth. Marina moved quickly, and didn't mind working in the castle or in the village, giving the castle scraps to the poor, clothing the beggars. She was free when she left the castle. Daphne was never free.

Daphne often wondered why Geovana might not demand her son's wife be so accomplished—rather than skilled at the dispersal of laundry—but there was simply no understanding the Countess. Especially since it so often seemed that *she* ruled Lendo, rather than Daphne's father, Pietro, who, taken alone, could be quite a pleasant man. She did love her father.

This morning, he had stopped by her bedroom, concerned by her illness of the night before. And so she had pleaded she was still weak and would remain abed, but did not need the doctor, just a day's rest.

And she had watched when first Marina, and then Armand, had hurried away from the castle, and up into the cliffs.

And she had followed.

And now . . . she hadn't even gotten to see what they were up to—and someone was coming!

In a panic, Daphne turned to run back down the hill.

Tripping on a rock, she lost a shoe. She tried to come to a quick halt and run back for it, but she froze instead. Armand had come into view, and was looking down at her quizzically.

"Well, hello!" she called cheerfully, her heart thundering.

"Daphne! Are you all right? Is something wrong? You . . . your father . . . ?"

"No, no, nothing is wrong!" she said quickly. She waved a hand toward her horse where it lazily ate grass, just twenty feet down the slope. "I . . ."

Words failed her. She shook her head.

"I had to get away for a bit," she said simply.

"Does your father know you're out?" he asked.

She shook her head. "I needed to get away," she said.

"I'd better get you back," he told her.

He whistled, and his horse came down the cliff, then followed him to where Daphne stood. Every animal obeyed him, she thought. He never used a whip, or an angry word, and all creatures seemed willing to follow his lead.

"My lady?" he said, offering her a boost up to her saddle.

She thanked him, and thought about his closeness to her as he performed the simple task. And when she was seated, she saw that he looked up at her, and the light in his eyes was so beautiful, so stirring.

"I would do anything, you know," he said very softly.

"Pardon?"

"I wake early daily, and train at arms. I will gladly go off to the wars, and prove myself. I would do anything to convince your father that I am the right man for you. And yet, I know . . . I know that I am the falcon master, and you are to wed the man who will be duke."

She was amazed at the tears that formed in her eyes, the tears she blinked back so quickly. "There's no way," she said softly, shaking her head. "There's no way . . . the wedding is in two weeks' time. At *Christmas*. It's too late."

"I would die for you," he said.

She reached down, curling her fingers around his. "And I will live, with this memory always. I will go through the years, knowing I had this moment, that you loved me."

She pulled her hand back and turned her horse.

Because there was no hope. And if her father knew about Armand's love . . .

If Geovana knew . . .

Then she would fear for his life.

Michelo awoke with a groan. He stared up at the sky, and saw that it was beautiful and blue, dotted with white clouds, and a glorious sun.

But at that moment, the sun only hurt his eyes. He closed them. As he did so, he heard a gasp. He tried to shade his eyes and open them again.

And when he did, he was dazzled.

Her hair, caught in the light, was the color of spun gold. She had the bluest eyes he'd ever seen. They rivaled the sky, the sea, the heavens.

And within those eyes . . . care, compassion, concern . . . tenderness.

"Are you all right?" A gentle hand touched his forehead, something cool. She had ripped her hem to dunk a piece of the fabric from her gown in the stream he could hear bubbling somewhere nearby. Her touch was smooth and soothing, ever so light upon his brow.

"Sir? No, of course, you're not all right. There's a gash on your temple, but . . ." She moved closer. He inhaled her scent. He saw the clean, classic lines of her face, and she might have been an angel, an ice princess, too lovely for the real world. "It's really not so bad. A surface wound. You're a warrior . . . you've been off to the borders?" she asked. "Wait, please, I'm so sorry. You needn't answer any questions. Let me help you . . . see if you've any other injuries. Can you rise, with my help?"

He looked at her solemnly. "I will definitely need your help."

"I'm here, and quite strong, actually," she assured him.

He put his arm around her shoulder. If he staggered as he rose, it would be because he couldn't tear his gaze away from her eyes.

"It's all right. Honestly. I have you." She flashed him a smile. He gained his balance, and yet did not want to let her slip from his hold. "Just a few steps . . . the brook is here. With clear, fresh, water. You must be very thirsty. I haven't a cup or anything to offer you."

"It's all right," he said. "Thank you."

At the brook, she helped him down to his knees. He bent over, splashing his face with the water, then drinking it in. It was refreshing, wonderful, cool, bathing away the confusion of the night, even the pain in his head.

No . . . it wasn't the water that had done that. The pain had faded, disappeared, the moment he had seen her eyes.

His thirst sated, his head cleared, he sat back by the water's edge, looking at her, marveling at her, wondering if she wasn't just an invention of his subconscious mind, a sprite to wake him gently after his fall. But she was there before him, those eyes still so brilliant, still so kind. And her hair! The wealth of it, touched by the sun.

"Thank you so much," he said.

"If you're a warrior returning, I can help get you home. Now, you are on one of the bluffs above the valley at the base of the castle at Lendo. Baristo is to the west, and to the northeast, the lands of the great Fiorelli. But you needn't fear if you are lost at all; I will gladly help you back."

"I'm not lost," he said, but then he wondered if he was. Not in place, not here, on these familiar bluffs. But lost in his future, and his purpose.

"What's your name?" she asked softly.

He started to answer, but hesitated. He didn't want her to know who he was, not yet at any rate. He was suddenly not at all in a great hurry to get home.

There would be time enough for duty and responsibility when he did arrive.

She leaned forward, touching his head with worry. "You must have struck your head quite hard. I should get you to a physician."

"No . . . no, there's no real harm. I think I just need time."

"You don't remember your name?" Thankfully, she didn't really give him time to answer. "I'll have to call you something, you know." She grinned. "You really are quite the warrior, you know, rather handsome. Perhaps, for now, we can just consider you to be Prince Charming."

"And you, my lady, beyond a doubt, I shall have to call Angel."

She inclined her head. "I shall accept, thank you. You poor fellow, truly. Any man who risks his life going to the borders . . . well, you are a prince charming, whatever your name and place may be. Is it terrible there?" she queried.

"We hold our own," he said.

She leaned against a rock at his side. He heard a sudden cawing sound, and turned to see that there was an outstandingly beautiful *falcon*, not a hundred yards from them. Bandages surrounded the animal's wing.

"A falcon," he murmured.

"Yes," the woman said lightly.

"She's injured." He arched a brow to her. "So you seek out all manner of wounded creatures in the hills?" he asked.

His *Angel* walked over to the falcon, gently touching her wing. "Poor thing, such an exquisite creature, and she was hurt by a hunter's arrow."

"Why would a hunter seek out a *falcon*?" he asked.

"Some men are simply killers, and they care not what they hunt," she murmured. "Isn't she lovely?"

"A beautiful creature," he agreed. "You seem to have a way with her, with all manner of beings, I imagine."

"Oh, yes! I am a falcon mas—" She cut herself off quickly, glancing his way with a rueful grin. "I think that they are magnificent creatures. And she is healing. And you . . . I wonder how I can help you. What might bring back your memory."

He came to his feet, a little unsteady.

"Oh, be careful!" she said.

"Walk with me a bit . . . perhaps I'll get my bearings."

"Gladly, sir. I will gladly walk with you."

Amazingly the falcon found the strength to flutter her wings and hopped upon his arm. The three set off for a walk in the ancient forest along the cliffs together.

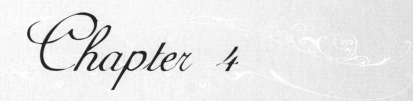

Chapter 4

Never, ever, would Marina doubt the word of Thomasina, the falcon, again.

The man she walked beside was everything she had asked for, and more.

He had not injured his head so badly as it had first appeared, and so they spent time just walking the beautiful landscape, traversing some of the little bridges that crossed the streams, finding high tors, and little copses where trees gave shade from the sun, and nature created the most beautiful dens. They talked about horses at first, and Marina, anxious to help, described the wonders of Calasia, the way the mountains fell to the sea, how lovely the aqua waters could be, and how the landscape with the jagged hills and then higher mountains had provided the bases for castles to be hewn into rock, and the deep valleys where rich earth allowed farmers to plow and grow the richest crops.

They came upon Radifini by the ancient stones and pillars, and Marina fell ever further under the man's enchantment, because he was immediately courteous and kind to her dear, old friend. Radifini listened to the story about the bump on his head, stroked his beard, smiled at him, and seemed not to think it a serious thing that he didn't know his name, or quite where he should be going.

"All of us have to stop during life at some point, and think about who we are, and where it is we really want to be going," he said. The old wizard talked with them a while, then said there were things he simply must be doing, and he left them alone.

Marina said that knowing Radifini was part of what made her world here, this part of Lendo, so very special for her.

And her lost "prince" smiled.

He listened to her with wonder, and when she asked why he frowned, he admitted sadly that things were dangerous upon the border lands, that they encountered wartrolls frequently, and he was afraid that the people and rulers of Lendo and Baristo did not fully see the danger.

"They are real then, the wartrolls?" she asked him. "You've captured one?"

He shook his head. "I've battled them often enough. And they are real—just as your falcon is real. Except she is one form of natural magic and beauty. Wartrolls are magical and evil. They do not die, as mortal men do. They are large, great hulking fellows. And they endure blow after blow . . . I don't know if they truly have scales for skin, like an armor. And I don't know if they can survive with injuries ten times greater than we can bear. But I've seen them rise when a man could not do so."

"If the stories about the wartrolls are true," she murmured, "then perhaps it's true that a great dragon lives somewhere near, high in its den, in these hills."

"The dragon," he said, and leaned closer to her. "I've heard tales of the dragon. They say that it is winged, magnificent, and terrible."

She smiled wistfully. "Indeed. According to legend, dragons had not been seen for years, and then, when Count Nico d'Or was just about to marry the Princess Elisia, the dragon appeared to sweep her away. But they were deeply, truly in love, devoted to one another. And Nico would gladly have given his life for her. He rode alone, into the hills, and he fought the dragon with the strength of a hundred men and brought her home."

"It's a pretty tale," he told her, smiling.

"It might well be true!" she said.

"He fought a dragon—alone?" he teased.

"I believe it might have been true."

"How could he have the strength of a hundred men?"

"Love, courage, and conviction can give a man, or woman, the strength of hundreds."

It was then he reached out to touch her face, marveling at the line of bone, the softness of her skin. And the belief in her eyes, those blue pools of sea and sky. She gave him a smile, a curl of amusement that was still touched by determination and the most beguiling inner belief and therein, strength.

And it was then he said, "I have never met anyone as wonderful as you."

Her smile deepened, and she said, "You are my one wish, my greatest desire, and just this day . . ."

"It cannot end here," he said, forgetting his father's commitment for him.

She didn't reply. She looked to the sky rather, and said, "I would dare the day, and the night, and be grateful for the magic within them."

"The sun is setting," he noted.

"And I should be gone," she murmured.

He caught her hand. "But you won't leave me?"

"Not this night."

And so, they found bounty from the land, the water that bubbled in the stream, fruits from the trees, berries from the brush, and though he was obviously a well-honed warrior, he seemed satisfied with what they ate. Marina herself didn't think she could find hunger for anything more than his mere presence when she was in his company.

She didn't know what would be happening in the court at Lendo, and that night, she didn't care. She would endure whatever the future brought, for this one night.

The sun fell and they stayed together, finding shelter against the cliffs and rocks. And they mused that one particularly high tor with dark caves might be the one where the dragon slept, if indeed, there was a dragon.

They talked, and they rested, and they touched. They lay together beneath the stars.

Marina held tight to every moment; she savored each word he said. She knew she would remember forever his eyes, and how they touched upon hers, the sound of his voice, and indeed, the scent that was his, the presence, the very vibrance and vitality that was life, and love.

She thought, when she awoke in the morning, he would be gone, that her dream, and her wish, would have vanished. But, as striking in sleep as he was when awake, he still lay at her side.

The sun was up. A new day had dawned. And the dream was over.

She rose. Moving away from the cliff where they had spent their night, she crept carefully, silently, and returned to the stream.

Thomasina, drinking at the stream, saw her and said, "A wish well spent?"

"A dream realized," Marina told her, and leaned to kiss the falcon gently upon the head. "Your wound . . . ?"

"Nearly healed," Thomasina said.

"Then I must go."

But she could not leave so quickly. She tiptoed back to her sleeping Prince Charming. She watched him a moment, her heart beating too quickly, and she knew that whatever came, she would always have this memory.

And she would love him forever.

She turned, as he was stirring, and ran down the cliff until she found Arabella, then made her way home.

Michelo awoke, and was stunned to find his Angel gone. The beautiful falcon, like a touch of magic, remained, and he looked at her, shaking his head. "How could she leave me?" Rising, he came to the falcon and carefully unwrapped the bandages. The injury was all but healed, and so he removed the binding completely. "Now, beautiful creature, you can fly free," he murmured. "If only it were so easy. Has she run free, as well?"

The falcon watched him sagely as he strode the area of the stream and the cliff, searching for her—his angel. At last, he saw something on the grass on the downward slope to the valley. Hoping it would give him some clue to the identity of his beloved, he hurried to see what it might be.

A shoe.

A delicate shoe, small, in gold satin.

As he studied the shoe, he heard a sound. Battle with the wartrolls had made him quick and alert. In fact, he wondered how he hadn't awakened when she had left him, and rued the fact that the one time he should really need to awaken at the slightest whisper of sound, he had not.

There was no danger. It was the old man, Radifini, coming down to join him.

"She's gone, sir. I have discovered the love of my life, and she is gone. All of these years, I have fought for these lands, never really understanding why honor was so dear, and now . . . I know that it is people, not land, that makes the fight, and love, not glory, that makes the warrior."

"Ah, young Michelo, you are a romantic, as well as a warrior," Radifini said.

"You know who I am?"

"Of course," Radifini said.

"You didn't betray me," Michelo said ruefully.

"Ah, well, there is who you are, and then, there is *who* you are. And you both needed to know the real *who* of one another, so . . ."

"Then who is she?" Michelo asked.

"The stepdaughter of Pietro d'Artois, Count of Lendo. Stepsister to the one you are to wed."

Michelo stared at him with horror and misery dawning.

"She is the betrothed of Carlo, Count Baristo," Radifini continued.

Michelo rose, bearing the shoe. "There is a way to change this. I'll go to my father. He is a great believer in magic and omens—after all, he was alive in the time when the Dragon in the Den supposedly appeared, and kidnapped the Princess Elisia!" Michelo plotted quickly. "I'll tell him that . . . my heart belongs to the owner of the shoe. I will slip it on her foot . . . and declare that it is an omen, that we must be together!"

"Good young sir! I fear that you are underestimating Carlo Baristo!" Radifini told him.

"He cannot love her. He cannot love her as I do!" Michelo swore.

"Well, I bid you good fortune then. I also caution you to take great care. And if, perchance, you should discover you need the aid of an old wizard, well, you know where I can be found," Radifini said gravely, and turned and walked away.

With his shoe, and his destiny set in his own mind, Michelo knew it was time to head for home.

Carlo was in a rage, which was not a pretty thing.

He had his father's bluster and the streak of evil that only his mother held in greater supply.

At his own castle in Baristo, he paced before the great fire. "They have told me—my spies have told me—that she didn't come in at all last night! She'll concoct a lie, of course, but she stayed out—in the hills. She loathes me—mocks me! Me—Carlo, Count of Baristo! The wretched girl. How can I marry such a young woman? She defies me; she thinks that she will say and do as she pleases!"

Geovana liked Marina even less than her son did—after all, she was the child of the falcon master-who-never-should-have-been-count *and* the wretched Princess Elisia, for whom men had gone to war, and all adored.

"It has never been the plan that you should stay married, Carlo. You need but walk with her to the altar, make her your bride, and then . . ."

"And then?" Carlo demanded of his mother.

And Geovana smiled her lovely, serene smile and said sweetly, "My son! Terrible things have been known to happen here! Great rocks—flying into bedrooms. And then, of course, there is the dragon."

"The dragon! Bah. If there was a dragon, it hasn't appeared in years!"

"Oh, but there is a dragon. And it will appear—if summoned," Geovana said, still calm, amused. "You will marry—for Lendo. And when it is yours, joined with Baristo . . . well, those lands will be greater than those owned by the great Duke Fiorelli!"

Smiling, Geovana left him, heading for her balcony (where, it was still whispered, she had the power to raise the elements, wind and fire, earth and water. And, perhaps, the dragon.)

The great Duke Orisini Fiorelli was really a very good man. He was a cheerful man, as well, one who loved his wife and was grateful for his children. He woke each morning in a good mood, and as was his custom, he walked to his balcony that morning, ready to start the day by waving to any of his people who might be down below. Though he was a little concerned that his son had not appeared as yet, he had deep faith in the boy, and would never believe that Michelo could have fallen on his way home.

That morning, he yawned and stretched, and looked around, but saw no one. He was about to return to his bedchamber when he saw something, perched on his balcony rail, that caught his astonished attention.

A falcon. Shimmering in the morning light. A magical creature, he thought with awe.

"How lovely you are! How I would love to own you, gorgeous creature. But then, you look as if you are the wind, freedom itself, so . . . I shall just admire you!"

Then, he could have sworn that it talked! Words came to him, as if carried softly on the wind.

"Oh, great Duke! Orisini Fiorelli of Calasia! You are the man with the greatest power, and the greatest responsibility!"

"Is my conscience talking to me?" he gasped. "Where have I failed?"

"Today, in the square at Lendo, you must not allow the future to be set without thought! I will come, and drop an olive branch before the lady who must become the bride of your son. Wrong can wear the face of right. But, you, great duke, must not be fooled!"

The falcon flapped its wing in the air. Then it turned, soared into the sky, and disappeared over the hills. Orisini stared after it. Amazed, and fearing his years were taking a toll on his mind, he shook his head. He returned to his bedroom, where his wife was stirring.

He sat on the edge of the bed. "I saw a falcon. It talked to me," he said.

"That's nice, dear," she said, still half-asleep.

"A falcon . . . my conscience!" He stood, determined. "That's what will be done!" he exclaimed.

His wife woke in full, blinking with confusion. "What will be done?" she asked.

"Today . . . in the square at Lendo. We will assemble all the ladies of Calasia in full. A falcon will come, and drop an olive branch. And Michelo must marry the girl who stands where the branch is dropped!"

He started out of the room. His wife, fully awake, jumped out of bed. "Orisini! There are bats flying about in your head, my love! The marriage is arranged. The invitations to the wedding are printed! There is to be a great feast . . . It will be Christmas Day! Orisini!" she wailed.

But he was gone.

And she sighed. The printers were going to just be furious!

Michelo came home to jubilation. The people greeted him even as he approached his house, and he greeted them with pleasure in return. At last, he walked into his parents' home, the great castle in the heart of Calasia. His mother, on the staircase, ran down, crying his name, eager to embrace him. His younger sister, growing now into womanhood herself, raced to him, and he lifted her, and swung her about with happiness. He kissed and hugged his mother, and then his father came, too, and for several minutes, they did nothing other than rejoice in one another's company.

Then, of course, his father asked about the situation on the borders, and Michelo gravely informed him that it was serious, and they must rally the people of Lendo and Baristo, and make them see the danger. His father listened solemnly, and agreed, but then staunchly decided they wouldn't speak of such things just yet.

"I have something to say, Father," Michelo told Orisini.

"And so do I!" his father said.

His mother groaned.

"It's about the wedding," Orisini said.

Again, Michelo's mother groaned.

"I have something to say, as well," Michelo told them.

"It's not to be so simple," Orisini explained.

"No, it cannot be, for I am in love," Michelo informed.

"In love!" his mother gasped.

"In love! How wonderful!" Adriana exclaimed. Naturally, his sweet young sister would understand.

"Perhaps you should go to your room," Lucia said worriedly to Adriana.

"Mother! And miss this?" Adriana protested, eyes sparkling.

"No one should miss love," Michelo said, grinning at his sister.

"Bah, love!" his father said.

"Orisini!" his mother protested, outraged.

"Well, dear, it's blessed that we are in love!" Orisini said, speaking quickly. "But our marriage was arranged."

She rolled her eyes, looking at her son. "Hear how he intends to arrange this!"

"Yes, son, we shall all go to the square in Lendo. Every lady in all of my dukedom of Calasia will assemble there. When the olive branch falls—"

"When the olive branch falls!" Michelo interrupted, astounded. "No, no, no, Father. You listened, I know, but you didn't hear me. I am in love. I know the girl I will wed."

"You know this girl?" his mother asked.

"I met her in the hills. You see, I did have a bit of an accident on the way home—I hit my head. And when I awoke, she was there."

"A dream girl, no more," his father said impatiently.

"You hit your head, dear," his mother said. "Obviously, you're well enough now . . . but she might well have been a dream, indeed."

"She was real! I have her shoe!" Michelo said, and produced it.

"Really. A dream girl would never lose a shoe," Adriana said, quite practically.

Orisini ignored them both. "When the olive branch falls—"

"Father—"

"When the olive branch falls—"

"How will this olive branch fall?" Michelo demanded.

"A falcon will drop it," Orisini said.

"A falcon spoke to him," his mother said, rolling her eyes once again.

"A falcon?" Michelo repeated.

"Yes, dear, a falcon," his mother said with a sigh.

"A *falcon*?" Michelo repeated.

"Why, yes! A falcon," Orisini said, delighted since it appeared that Michelo understood.

A falcon? Could it be . . .

Michelo had seen wartrolls. And he had seen the beautiful falcon in the woods. A creature so very magnificent that surely . . .

Perhaps, myth and magic could be true.

"Let's see what happens," he told his father cautiously.

Pietro d'Artois, Count of Lendo, fumed in astonishment. "It's changed!" he swore angrily. His daughter stood before him, staring at her father. "I don't believe this insult, this indignity! Now, the great Fiorelli claims we must all stand out in the square, that there has been an omen, that for the good of all the lands, we must gather and wait—and a *falcon* will decide our fates!"

Daphne listened, barely able to believe her good fortune. "Then—I'm not to marry Michelo Fiorelli?" she whispered.

He glanced at her, dismayed and despairing that she should find such pleasure in this disaster. "The wretched falcon could drop the olive branch before you," he reminded her. "In fact, it must, it must . . . I will consult Geovana, that's what I'll do!" he said.

Before she could stop him, her father left her.

"Yes!" she cried out when he was gone. "Oh, yes! Please, please, falcon—or whatever you may be! Whatever you do, don't drop that branch before me!"

If not for the fact that Armand had heard about the happenings in the courtyard, Marina herself might have never known what was going to happen. Apparently, a crier had gone out, informing all the ladies of Calasia they must be in the square at sundown, for the great Duke Fiorelli had been given an omen, and his

son would marry only when a falcon had dropped an olive branch before the girl he was intended to wed.

Michelo Fiorelli had been wounded, and he had just made it home after a night out on the cliffs.

And so she knew.

Michelo had been her dream prince. The great duke's son—previously to marry her stepsister—was now destined to follow a new plan of his father's.

Somehow, that plan involved a falcon.

Hope took flight inside her. There could be no other falcon to deliver such an omen than her own dear Thomasina.

Armand's excitement was contagious. But even as they whispered in the courtyard, Geovana called sharply to Marina from her chamber above.

"Come up here, now! Ungrateful girl!" Geovana cried down angrily.

"I'd best go," Marina murmured. She didn't want to fight with Geovana. Nor did she dare show her excitement.

But when she went upstairs and met the woman—who really had no business in Marina's own poor chambers—she was to be severely shaken by the news delivered to her. "There is to be some nonsense in the square today. Naturally, I must be there. However, you are engaged to Carlo. So you will stay here, and see that all is set when we return to the castle for the feast we must have prepared to follow the silliness old Orisini has decreed."

"But . . . I was of the understanding that every lady was to be there!" Marina protested.

Geovana looked down her nose at Marina, and suddenly, her hatred was so apparent in her eyes that Marina nearly recoiled from it.

"You! You! No, my girl, no! You will be Carlo's wife. You ungrateful wench! You are nothing but the daughter of an upstart falcon master, and you should be on your knees with gratitude that a man such as my son even considers you to be his wife!"

"Geovana, the great Duke Fiorelli—"

"Is addled! Senile. You will stay here!" She wagged a finger at her. "You will stay here and obey me. You know, child, that great rocks have been known to fly about this place!"

"I must be there," Marina said determinedly. She headed to the door.

To her amazement, Geovana set her hands upon her shoulders, wrenching her back. She did so with such strength Marina was amazed. She flew back against the wall, barely maintaining her balance.

"You!" Geovana said, pointing at her with repugnance. "You!"

She said no more.

She turned and left through Marina's door, slamming it in her wake.

Marina stood still for a minute, shaken by the intensity of the hatred the woman had shown her.

But she would not stay. Somehow, Thomasina, the falcon, had managed to give her far more than her second wish. She was trying to give her a far greater gift—a chance at a real life.

She walked to her door, determined she would get out and disappear at that moment.

Her door, she discovered, was locked. Bolted from the outside.

She cried out and banged against it, then stopped. No one would come. No one in the household would dare defy Geovana.

Trying to calm herself, she walked to the balcony and looked down. Armand was gone.

They had probably tied him up somewhere, lest he cause trouble!

No one was about.

But she had to be in the courtyard! There must be a way.

The fall to the ground would be . . . deadly.

Marina went back to her room and sat at the foot of the bed, thinking. She had one more wish left. And yet . . . to use it would leave her with nothing if worse things were to happen.

She had to help herself.

And yet . . . *how?*

She walked to the balcony again and looked down, judging the distance. She paced back into her room, and began to strip the sheets from the bed, tying them together.

She ran back to the balcony, throwing her makeshift rope over to judge the distance anew. There would still be a fall, and yet . . .

Oh, dear God! She had to risk it!

She was just about ready to take the chance when her door suddenly opened.

Chapter 5

here wasn't much time.

Geovana hurried to her own balcony, where she kept a great cauldron. There, she threw into it the items necessary for any great spell.

Eye of newt.

Horn of toad.

And so forth, and so forth.

At last, her great potion was steaming. She cast out her arms, and spoke the words.

And she drank deeply . . .

Then she carefully took a bit of time—naturally, she had to be attired in her best—and hurried back to Lendo.

Let the old fool Orisini bring on a falcon!

"Daphne!" Marina gasped. She nearly threw her bedsheet-rope-ladder right over the balcony window; she had been caught red-handed.

"What are you doing?" Daphne demanded.

"Nothing!"

Daphne laughed softly. "You might have killed yourself!"

"And I might have gotten down safely."

"At any rate, it isn't necessary," Daphne said quickly. "Geovana had to go back to Baristo for some reason. She ordered that the servants go nowhere near these doors, and she forced poor Armand to ride with her. But no one ordered me not to open the door, so . . ."

Marina stared at her stepsister for a long moment. "I'm in love with the man who is supposed to be your husband," she said quickly.

And to her amazement, Daphne smiled. "Then let's pray the silly branch falls in front of you!"

"You . . . don't want to be the wife of the great Duke Fiorelli's son?" Marina inquired carefully.

"Good heavens, no! Oh, I'm sure he is a decent fellow. But I . . . oh, I am hopelessly in love with Armand!"

Marina gasped with pleasure, flying across the room to hug Daphne. "Oh, you've no idea how he adores you!" she said, and Daphne flushed.

"I think I have an inkling," she murmured. "But . . . that is probably a truly hopeless quest. And yet, if I can just avoid having to marry Michelo Fiorelli . . ."

"I will leap to the heavens to catch that olive branch!" Marina swore, and she started out of the room. Then she paused. "No, I must wait. Hide somewhere until the last minute. Or else . . . she will find a way to stop me from being there. Geovana will stop me."

"My room!" Daphne said, after a moment's thought. "Then, when it is time . . ."

Marina smiled, looking at her. "All these years!" she said softly. "We've barely brushed by one another, and yet . . . well, you are the finest sister!"

"And I have envied you, when I just wanted to have more of your strength!" Daphne told her.

"Somehow, I will help you. You and Armand," Marina swore.

"Hurry then, I must get out here, and you must time things well!" Daphne said.

"Yes, always, we must help ourselves—and be grateful for aid from others!" Marina agreed, and they were arm in arm as they snuck out of her room, careful lest they should be seen by any other.

Arriving with great fanfare in Lendo, riding with his wife, daughter, and son, Orisini was glad to greet the people, and he was glad, too, of the air of happiness and excitement around him. The people were pleased their great overlord would consider them all when seeking to find a bride for his son.

Minstrels played, music abounded. The path was strewn with flowers where their horses trod, and the people called out, hailing Michelo. Michelo, his dear son, true to his blood, responded in good nature, reaching down to touch hands, to thank those who applauded him.

He saw Pietro awaiting him, Geovana at his side, at the steps down to the great square. Carlo Baristo was there, as well, as he should be. And in the square, with many other fair young maidens, was Daphne, the beautiful, accomplished daughter of Pietro. There was another girl, Orisini thought with a frown. Dear Nico and Elisia's daughter. She was nowhere to be seen. But he'd heard she was something of an eccentric, never attending state functions, always preferring to run about in the hills. Ah, well! Pietro had told him she would be wed to Carlo, so . . .

All about . . . people danced and sang, making way for him and his party.

They came to the center.

"Pietro! Geovana! Carlo!" he cried.

And, of course, as was their way, once he had dismounted, they all greeted one another with warm affection, hugging, kissing on both cheeks.

"Well, Orisini, this is an interesting piece of business you've devised," Pietro told him.

Orisini smiled. "It's what must be. We shall see if we have all envisioned the future as it should be for our children."

He turned back to see his son. To his consternation, it appeared that Michelo was looking anxiously through the crowd.

"She isn't here."

"Who?"

"The girl I will wed."

"Son! We agreed that where the olive branch falls . . ."

"Father, we didn't exactly agree—"

"Look! See, it is true! There is a falcon, a beautiful falcon! Magic does exist; I am not in my dotage!

Here comes the falcon!"

The people began to ooh and aah. Michelo saw everyone was looking through the square with amazement—his father's certainty that a falcon would come was being proven to be true. Pietro was staring at the creature with a frown, Carlo with anger, and Geovana . . .

Was suddenly nowhere to be seen.

Michelo looked around anxiously. Indeed, the beautiful falcon he had first seen by the stream was now flying through the square.

But his angel of the night was nowhere to be seen.

He gritted his teeth. *No, no, no . . . !*

Then he saw her. She came streaking out from the courtyard of the castle, agile, graceful, running . . . seeming to slip through the crowd like a wisp of smoke. She hurried to where Daphne stood, along with all the young women of the dukedom and counties. She and Daphne smiled, embraced, and stepped apart.

His heart seemed to thunder and tremble in his chest. The falcon was an omen, a true touch of magic, and she would set things straight. She flew over the crowd, an olive branch held lightly in her beak. She had come to help them; all would be well.

And then . . .

Suddenly, there was a dragon.

A dragon, yes, huge and snarling, its smoke-infused cry so loud and piercing that people screamed out with dismay, stepping back. As the falcon dove downward, the dragon tore through the crowd, flying low, its terrible tail whipping about, as it zigged and zagged, furiously going after the incredible falcon. The falcon flew hard, heading straight for Marina d'Or. But the dragon, creating fear and panic in the crowd, was nearly atop the falcon.

The falcon let forth a caw.

The olive branch dropped as the falcon burst forward with speed, but then veered, and flapped her wings into a furious soar, the heinous, huge dragon at her heels.

The olive branch fell directly between Marina and Daphne.

The people began to murmur, and many trembled as they stepped forward again, watching the falcon and dragon disappear up the hill, and into the forest.

Suddenly, the falcon, the dragon still hard upon her, rose and fell, clawing at the dragon.

And they could all hear the cry of rage and pain that the dragon let out, falling back. As they all watched in silence, the falcon flew on.

For several minutes, the wind blew, and it was all the sound in the world as the people watched, sighing with relief as the falcon appeared alive and well and uninjured on the crest of another peak.

"It was a dragon!" someone called out. "There *is* a dragon!"

"A dragon!" someone else repeated with horror.

"And a falcon!" Duke Orisini announced, his voice strong.

The people moved forward again, all staring at the olive branch on the ground, fallen between the two stepsisters.

Again, there was silence, as moments ticked away.

"It is before Daphne, as it should be!" Pietro exclaimed.

"Indeed, exactly!" came the strong sound of a woman's voice.

As Michelo walked forward himself, he saw that Geovana was there. Her headdress was a bit askew, and she looked winded and flustered. She was bent slightly, as if she had a pain in her ribs. But she was right there, with them, insisting that the branch was closer to Daphne.

His father was at his side. "Wait!" he implored. "There must be a measurement. Where is the ducal measurer?"

Michelo stood in silence as they waited. Marina's eyes touched his, blue as the sea, as the sky, and he stared back with all the love in his heart.

The ducal measurer arrived, and with consternation, rose to inform them all that the olive branch lay exactly between the two girls.

The great Duke Orisini Fiorelli was silent. Michelo stepped forward, producing the satin slipper. "Father, this is the shoe of the woman I will marry. It will fit the right foot."

He'd been so certain . . .

Then, he knew he was wrong as he saw the confusion that touched his beloved's face—and the horror that was reflected in Daphne's.

Still, he bent down before Marina. She leant over to whisper to him, "My feet are huge! I'm so sorry . . . that will never fit me."

And close to her, Daphne whispered. "It's mine! I lost it the other day. Good Lord, what will we do now?"

Marina, bending low, whispered in sorrow, "I am so . . . so sorry. Daphne is right! What will we do now? I suppose the wife of a duke's son should have dainty feet . . . mine are just . . . big!"

"There, the shoe fits Daphne!" Geovana cried loudly.

"No!" Michelo cried. "I am in love with Marina, the child of the late and beloved Nico, and his princess bride, Elisia."

"And I am in love with Michelo!" Marina vowed, looking with love into his eyes, that he should declare his devotion there, in the square, before his father, his mother, and everyone.

"And I'm in love with Armand!" Daphne cried, bravely stepping forward with her conviction.

Pietro d'Artois gasped, turned red, and looked as if he would have apoplexy.

"I love Daphne!" Armand shouted, pushing his way through the crowd.

But before he could do more than come near, there was the sudden sound of a horrible explosion in the air.

It was like thunder, and it was as if lightning lit up the sky.

And there, above them all, was the dragon again.

Now there was time to really see the being, to study it.

Huge, beautiful in its ferocity, multicolored, with evil-glowing yellow and gold eyes, it soared above them, and the lightning was the fire of its breath, and the thunder the flap of its wings.

The people began to scream. After all, the dragon had been after the falcon. Now it was after them, invoking pure terror! The people ran in confusion, desperate for cover.

Jagged streaks of fire fell upon the square. Thatch-roofed shops went up in explosions of flame.

Michelo cast himself upon Marina, and they fell to the ground together. All around them, people screamed and ran.

Then, after raining down fire bolts and creating absolute mayhem, the dragon was gone.

Slowly . . . slowly, the people began to reappear in the square, murmuring about omens, and saying with fear that if there was good magic, such as the gorgeous falcon, it was natural that there should be bad magic.

Like the dragon.

The dragon—gone again. It was as if it had come, and then completely disappeared.

Michelo cried out, "We must be calm. Evil has been fought before; evil can be fought again!"

"Fought! What, shall we bring about the deaths of every man, woman, and child in all the land?" It was Geovana, naturally.

She walked to the center of the square and cast out her arms. She looked more disheveled even than she had before. In fact, quite frankly, she was something of a mess.

And yet she appeared . . .

Powerful. Her eyes were as gold as the dragon's, and her voice carried the thunder of the flapping of its wings.

"We have awakened the great Dragon in the Den! He is filled with rage. The old ways, the omens, have been invoked. Now, if any are to live, we must give him his due, his sacrifice!"

She whirled then, turning to the place where all four lovers had gathered together.

"The old ways have indeed been resurrected, and the result—that terrible dragon! As in the days of old, we must do our part. He must have a sacrifice, if anyone is to live, to survive! And his sacrifice must be the fairest damsel in the land. The woman who would be wife to the greatest leader, the greatest warrior. The woman who would wed Michelo, heir to the great Duke Fiorelli!"

There was a shuffling sound. It was Pietro d'Artois. He stepped forward, anxiously pushing the olive branch with his toe until it lay directly before Marina.

He wasn't a bad man, not really. But then, he'd been given a chance to give either his stepdaughter or his precious Daphne up to a dragon that meant to have her for dinner . . . literally!

"Marina!" he cried. "Alas!" And he either wept, or pretended to do so. "It must be Marina, child of Nico d'Or, who stole away the Princess Elisia when she was in the dragon's keeping. It must be Marina!"

"Aye, Marina!" cried someone in the crowd.

"No!" someone else protested.

"She must be given to the dragon—or else it will eat us all!" another voice roared.

"Wait a minute!" Michelo insisted. "What are you? Men—or mice? We will put together a hunting party. We will fight the dragon!"

"It should have been me!" Daphne said. "I am the upstart here, really!"

"Shut up, girl!" Pietro chastised her firmly.

Marina stepped forward. "Seriously! What are we? Cowards? Michelo is right. Appease the dragon once, and he will take everything from you. I will fight! We must all fight!"

"Men—or mice?" Michelo shouted again.

And a fellow, his cap in his hands, stepped forward. "To the dragon, great Michelo, I'm afraid that we are nothing but mice!"

"Duke Fiorelli! The dragon must be given his due!" another cried from the back of the crowd. Michelo thought that the voice sounded suspiciously like that of the Countess Geovana.

His father sighed deeply.

"We'll all die!" the miller's wife cried out.

"Duke, you must save us!" the baker himself pleaded.

Orisini Fiorelli looked at his son. He was obviously in great torment. "Michelo, I am sorry. The people come first," he said softly.

"No!" Michelo said.

But his father raised his voice. "Place my son under arrest. And God forgive us all, but . . . take the Lady Marina, and see that she is kept under lock and key and guard . . ."

"Father, no, no!" Michelo protested.

But the guards were racing around him, doing his father's bidding. He struggled, but there were too many, and in minutes, despite the black eyes and swollen jaws he doled out, he was in chains.

And when he looked across the square, Marina, calm, dignified, tall, and beautiful, was in chains, as well. Eyes meeting his.

She spoke to him, and the crowd, as a wistful smile touched her face. "I will not go easily!" she cried. "I will fight the dragon, when the time comes. I will fight it for myself—and for your daughters, because if you give in now, the dragon will demand more and more."

There was silence.

"This is foolish! You would think that we were living in the Dark Ages!" Marina cried.

Daphne cleared her throat and said softly, "We are living in the Dark Ages."

Marina shot her a quick glance, and nodded. "We must no longer live in the Dark Ages! We must find enlightenment in strength, in unity!"

"We will fight!" Michelo raged, straining against his shackles.

"They're right!" came another cry, and this time, it was the beautiful dance tutor, Serafina, who stepped forward. "We mustn't ever give into tyranny of any kind!" she cried. "Marina has spoken with such truth. If we give in now, the dragon will have us at its mercy. It will demand that we give in time and time again, and that we give in a little more each time. We must fight!"

But Geovana stepped forward. "Fight the dragon, and everyone will perish!" she proclaimed. "Take them away! Now!" she told the guards.

"Geovana, you must listen!" Serafina begged. Geovana offered a grim smile, and raised a hand, and guards rushed forward to seize Serafina. "See that she is banished," Geovana said sweetly, and lowered her head to offer a soft whisper to Serafina. "Return, and you will be the next sacrifice we offer to the dragon."

"Wait!" Michelo shouted, and began to fight again. But someone smote him on the head, and he discovered he was living in a personal dark age himself, for the light faded before his eyes, and he fell.

The following morning arrived with a brilliant sunrise.

"I'm quite confused," Radifini said, pacing the small confines of the deep, dark dungeon cell where Marina had been taken.

"You're confused?" Marina said. "I am about to become dragon chow, Radifini, and you are confused?"

He shook his head, stroking his beard as he walked. "There was a curse, you know. I thought perhaps it had been averted . . ."

"A curse? Dear Radifini, it seems that my life has been a curse!" she told him.

"Yes, yes . . . I'm quite sure that she put many curses on the house of d'Or."

"She?"

"Geovana, naturally. She was insanely jealous from the moment she heard about your mother, Marina, and she is quite powerful. But . . . rumor had it that the child of Nico and Elisia was to fall from a horse, crack her head on a rock, and fall into a deep and endless sleep. Naturally, when I heard this, I did my best to create counter-magic. I couldn't stop such a spell, but through my magic, I had it that after the crack on the head, the child should awaken at the slightest brush of love's true kiss!"

Marina sighed. "Radifini, I have never fallen from a horse. I haven't cracked my head, and I'm not asleep. I'm in a dungeon, about to be dragged up a cliff, tied to a stake—and left to be charbroiled by a dragon's fiery breath, and savored as supper."

"Yes, yes, that's how it appears," Radifini murmured.

He smiled at her. "Maybe! Just maybe, you'll fall off the horse while you're being taken up the cliff!"

Marina stared at him. "Radifini, I do love you, but . . . I think I need to think much more deeply to get out of this situation."

"Well, if you are to be charbroiled and consumed, it would be best if you were in a deep and endless sleep when it occurred, don't you think?"

"Radifini!" Marina protested. She began to pace the cell herself. "Armand is in chains, Michelo is in chains . . . and I am here." She paused. "There is my third wish. I can just wish—!"

"No, no!" Radifini protested, putting up a hand to prevent her from speaking any more words. "You must save the wish for a very last resort."

"I may be on my last resort right now," she reminded him.

He shook his head. "Wishes can come true, but the way they come true might not be to the very best good."

"Wishing myself *not* to be eaten by a dragon seems rather good to me," Marina commented.

Radifini shook his head. "Such a wish could put Daphne in your place. Or mean that all of Calasia is swept by a firestorm. Or that some other terrible event occurrs. Yes, you have your third wish. But you must keep and guard that wish until there is no other choice."

They heard the sound of heavy footsteps, coming along the dungeon path.

The guards of Pietro d'Artois came into the barred cell, pushing Radifini firmly aside, but with no malice.

The man in charge had tears in his eyes as he told Marina it was time. They were to climb the hills, and in front of the caves where the dragon had been reputed to sleep for all the years prior to yesterday's appearance, she was to be shackled to a post to await the dragon's whim—or appetite.

Marina listened to the decree.

One of the other guards fell to his knees. "Bless you, dear Lady Marina, that you make this sacrifice for us."

"Sir, get up!" she scolded him. "I intend to fight the dragon!"

They all looked at her sadly. Rather hard to fight a dragon, shackled to a post.

They led her from her cell, out from the bowels of the castle, and to the square, where Pietro read another decree, and even he had tears in his eyes. Real tears, she thought. He wasn't such a bad man. He was simply under Geovana's power.

Marina could only shake her head with impatience—growing desperation—and another passionate plea that they fight.

"Stepfather! People of Lendo, and all of Calasia! There is no appeasing a monster, don't any of you see this? The dragon will taste blood, and want more!"

This didn't seem to assure or inspire any of them, and though the good people around her continued to weep and sob, they saw to it that she was mounted upon Arabella, and the solemn ride up the cliff began.

She was alone, she thought. Radifini had been shoved back and left behind when the guards had come. Armand and Michelo remained imprisoned. Even Daphne had been locked away somewhere, to prevent her from rousing the people.

And yet, as they neared the cliffs, Marina heard the thunder of hooves.

And the falcon, Thomasina, came to fly alongside Arabella as they rode.

"You have your third wish!" the falcon reminded her.

"Radifini warned me that I must use it as a last resort, lest I take the chance of bringing harm to others," Marina said softly. The guards stared at her. They were aware, of course, that the magical falcon had come to ride with them, but they could not hear her speak, and so they thought that Marina was losing her mind.

But since she was about to be fed to a dragon, that didn't seem like such a bad thing.

"Radifini is wise," Thomasina concurred. "Remember, wishes are what we dream in our hearts, and of course, we must always help ourselves!" If a bird could offer a dry smile, it seemed that Thomasina did then. "Remember. It's nearly Christmas. It's a time of belief, and belief is in the heart."

"I believe the dragon is about to help itself," Marina murmured.

Thomasina suddenly flew from her, heading to a distant plateau. As she rode, Marina began to mull the question of how best to use her last wish, taking care that her freedom from the jaws of the dragon didn't imperil the life of someone else. She smiled, remembering what both Thomasina and Radifini had told her. Christmas. A time of real magic in the heart and soul. A time of true gifts to all men—and women—of good faith.

She must be strong, and remember.

Suddenly, as they rounded a bend, a creature darted from the brush.

It was a skunk! A shimmering, almost silver, albino skunk!

Arabella reared up high, spooked.

Marina, with her hands tied behind her back, could not keep her seat in the saddle.

She was thrown from the horse's back.

She landed hard upon the ground, hit her head on a rock, and was out cold.

The guards, who had all heard rumors about such a curse, gathered round her.

"This is it!" one cried. "The deep and endless sleep!"

And another worried, "What shall we do?"

"Bring her before the cave, and leave her as we were commanded," the first guard decided.

"But . . . is a dragon like a reptile?" one asked. "With certain reptiles . . . well, they like their meals alive and warm and moving about. Snakes . . . certain snakes will only go for wiggling, moving prey!"

So they all argued among themselves, wondering if their great sacrifice to the dragon was still worthy.

But then the head man of the guard gave a great sigh. "Our poor, valiant, Lady Marina! Let's be grateful she is in a deep and endless sleep. Then she will not know . . ."

He didn't finish his sentence. They'd all seen the dragon. And they wept again as they picked up Marina, thinking that the curse was actually a blessing.

Their precious lady would not see when she became their ultimate sacrifice.

In time, she was taken before the cave of the Dragon in the Den, and before it, as decreed, she was bound to a stake.

The guards, certain they heard heavy breathing, and the rasp and cackle of fire from within, hurried with their task.

And then, they hurried with even greater energy to depart from the dragon's arena.

Chapter 6

All this time, Marina's friends and her beloved, Michelo, had not been sitting idle.

Yes, in chains, but not idle.

Michelo, being a warrior, and a hero, was being kept under guard.

But thinking that Armand was just the falcon master, a man who tilted with scarecrows and lost, Pietro had only ordered him kept in the dungeon, and even his chains had been loosely secured.

And so, through the night, he had slowly, persistently, worked at the chains, and by midmorning, he had caused them to slip from his wrists. As he reflected upon how best then to escape the bars of his dungeon cell, old Radifini came down the dank winding stairs, and hailed his guard, telling him that he had come to spend this time of the dragon with Armand, their dear lady's cousin. As Radifini spoke, Armand rose, seized the unwary guard's sword, and placed the point threateningly against the man's back. Though he protested, warning Radifini and Armand that they would bring about the demise of all if they were to interfere, the guard saw the immediacy of saving his own life as more important. He opened the barred door, entered the cell himself when his captors insisted, and was then locked away with a bump on the head so that he could not sound an alarm.

"And now . . . ?" Armand reflected.

"We must go for Michelo," Radifini said.

"There will be dozens of guards around him," Armand pointed out.

"Yes, that will be a problem," Radifini mused. And so, he paced again as he thought. But as he did so, there was a rustle in the corridor of the dungeons, and they looked up to see that Daphne was hurrying

toward them.

"Daphne!" Armand cried, and flew happily to her side, taking her into his arms with amazement. "How . . . ?"

"I learned a trick or two from my stepsister," she told him, and grinned. "I exited my chamber using my bedsheets and lowering myself into the garden."

For a moment, they marveled at her ingenuity. But then Radifini stopped them. "We must free Michelo."

And Daphne told them, "He is not heavily guarded. He is merely held back by chains of magic. I heard Geovana assuring my father that it would be so."

"Magic!" Radifini said with pleasure. And so, with Daphne in the lead, they hurried to the place where Michelo was kept.

He was rather sorry looking at that moment, hair disheveled, clothing torn, for he had tried again and again to break through the invisible bars holding him to the farthest, darkest, dankest wall in the deepest pit of the dungeons.

"Thank God!" he breathed when he saw them. "We must hurry!"

Radifini raised his hands, and began to thunder out words of magic. He nodded, pleased, to Michelo, who once again tried to step free.

But Michelo bounced back against the wall as he tried to move, as if struck by a giant hand.

"Radifini!" he cried.

"All right, all right, I'm rusty! It's been a long time since anyone has believed in magic here!" he told them.

He began another incantation.

And then another.

And finally—after both Armand and Daphne had been forced to sit, the wait growing very tiring, he said some words in an ancient tongue. "It's up to you now!" he implored Michelo.

Michelo stared at him. And then he said, "Before God, I love her more than life itself! I will save Marina! I have the strength, and I will break free from these chains of evil, slay the dragon, and rescue my bride!"

And with that, he burst free.

"Old man," Michelo said, "what words did you use that were finally the right ones?"

"Oh, I just spoke gibberish," Radifini told him cheerfully. "You spoke the words of magic! Love . . . emotion, the goodness in the heart and soul that is stronger than all else! Now—we must move quickly!"

High upon the highest cliff, the sleeping Marina remained bound to the post.

Thomasina, the falcon, had come to perch by her side, anxiously watching her.

And then . . .

The dragon appeared. It grinned an evil grin, for all had come to pass as the dragon desired, and the child of Nico and Elisia was there, for the taking.

But when the dragon, with all its power and brilliance, strode out for the sacrifice, the falcon let out a shrill caw of challenge, stretching out her wings, flying forward, ready to skewer the dragon through with her claws.

The dragon flew high, avoiding the talons.

The dragon had long awaited this day. It did not intend its sure destruction of Marina d'Or be disturbed; the dragon intended to savor every morsel. And so, it intended to see to the destruction of this new foe first.

The falcon must die.

The dragon flew, soared, glided, and attempted many times to breathe fire upon the falcon, or to slam it to the ground. But the falcon was swift and fleet, and though heavily beset, she evaded every attack.

Thus it was when the defenders arrived, Michelo in the lead, followed by Armand and Daphne.

Following them, of course, were others. The brave Antonio, Michelo's right-hand man, was there, back from the border as if he had known his mighty sword arm would be needed. Guards followed him from the castle, at his command—and because they had discovered their prisoners were gone. They were in confusion at first, for though Geovana and Carlo were not about, Pietro d'Artois was incredibly upset—if Marina was to escape, he feared for his own daughter's life. Antonio simply meant to be a defender in the righteous battle undertaken by his friend Michelo. They all quickly saw it was time to stand and fight.

As they reached the crest, Michelo drew forth both his sword and shield, anxious to rush forward and battle the dragon. But old Radifini stopped him, a hand upon his shoulder.

"Marina first!" he said.

"Old man, you must free her, as I fight the dragon," Michelo said.

To the amazement of all, Carlo Baristo, mounted on a great roan stallion, suddenly appeared on the cliff.

"I will save her!" he cried. He dismounted, heading straight for Marina. "I will kiss the lips of my beloved, and save her from the dragon! I am the man to do so!"

Now, they all doubted this very much. Carlo had been very angry with Marina, and if they had searched their hearts, all in Calasia would have known he had never intended to keep Marina as his bride for long.

"She is my beloved!" Michelo called angrily.

It was what Carlo wanted, of course. He smiled, and stepped forward, his sword swinging.

The two began a terrible battle. Swords clashed; steel sparks flew. The others fell back, watching their great fight with one another.

It was Daphne who noted the dragon was ignoring the two, and approaching the post where Marina slept, vulnerable to the attack.

"The dragon!" she told Armand, and they both rushed forward, dodging the shots of fire the dragon breathed, Armand trying very hard to pierce the armor of its scales with his sword, Daphne punching with all her strength.

The falcon, seeing everything in disarray and fearing the dragon's triumph, rushed in, coming between Michelo and Carlo Baristo. She flew high, then low, wings flapping, talons grasping at Carlo, causing him to stumble back and fall.

He, too, hit his head on a rock, and didn't rise.

"Is that fair, in magic?" Michelo asked softly.

The falcon cawed.

"The dragon, I must slay the dragon!" Michelo roared, seeing his friends at battle.

"No, you must kiss Marina," Radifini told him.

"There's a dragon to be fought!" Michelo protested.

"She sleeps! You must kiss her," Radifini argued. "Oh! When will you humans learn that love and compassion are far stronger than even the mightiest sword arm?"

Though Michelo loved Marina more than he knew a heart could bear, this made no sense. But Radifini was insistent, and so he ran first to the post where Marina was tied. The dragon attacked as he did so, but Radifini, flapping his arms as if he were a deranged bird himself, ran to the dragon, hitting it with all his strength in the nose.

The dragon roared, nearly singeing them all with its fiery breath.

"Can't you deliver a kiss quickly?" Radifini shouted.

Though it was not at all the deep and binding kiss a lover would give, Michelo quickly brushed his lips against Marina's.

And she awoke. Eyes wide and beautiful, as blue as the sea, as blue as the sky.

"Now fight the dragon!" Radifini begged, for the creature had drawn back, and pure evil and pleasure was in its eyes as it contemplated making a snack of Radifini.

Marina, awakened, struggled fiercely with her shackles. Armand and Daphne, relieved from their fight with the dragon, hurried over to help her. Between them, they freed her, and they hugged briefly as she spoke her gratitude.

But there, on the cliff, Michelo still fought valiantly against the dragon. Marina cried out softly, for the creature was very fierce, and it didn't seem that Michelo's sword was denting the scaly armor of the creature at all.

"Rocks!" she cried. "We must all throw rocks!"

They did. They created a fierce hail of stone, pelting the creature in a fury. It roared its anger, snapping here and there in a frenzy, yet held back by Michelo's sword. He must have penetrated the dragon's skin at some point, for flecks of blood flew from the dragon, and fell to the ground.

Where the blood drops landed, the earth itself began to rise, and every little speck of blood writhed and inflated until it became . . .

A wartroll.

Marina cried out with horror, warning them all.

And yet, as the newborn enemies advanced, the guards from the village at last began to arrive. So it was that the battle with the dragon became a great war, and the guards of Lendo realized at last that there was no appeasing such an enemy, and they began to fight. No man, woman, child, or even beautiful damsel in distress should ever be sacrificed to fear and tyranny.

It was a wicked and desperate battle. Yet with pride and purpose, they all held their own, fighting with what weapons they had, swords for some, rocks for others, dodging, feinting—running!—when all else failed.

Marina had gotten her hands on a sword and was very desperately fighting a wartroll herself when Radifini whispered in her ear, "Carlo lies there, beginning to rouse. You must go kiss him."

She was so stunned that she was nearly smote in two by the wartroll she battled. He had been right many times, but now, it seemed that poor Radifini had finally lost his senses.

"Kiss Carlo!" she exclaimed. "I'd as soon kiss a toad!"

With a lucky duck and blow, she was able to stop the wartroll who had so nearly done the dragon's work of dissecting her.

"Kiss Carlo. In life, there are times when we must kiss a few toads," he said calmly. "Then we know them clearly, for what they are."

He was dear; she loved him. But poor Thomasina was flying about in a frenzy, attempting to be a distraction; Michelo was still so desperately fighting the dragon; and the battle was going on all around her.

"Kiss him, quickly!" Radifini insisted.

And so, she lowered her sword, rushed to the area where Carlo lay, and knelt at his side.

He looked up at her, and she thought his eyes were evil, cold, and yellow-gold, like those of the dragon. And of his mother, Geovana.

His anger erupted as he looked at her. "Did you think I would have ever let you serve as ruler with me? Always, Marina, you were intended for the wrath of the dragon!"

"Kiss him, quick," Radifini commanded at her shoulder.

She shrugged. And she leaned down and kissed Carlo.

To her amazement, he began to bubble. Yes, bubble. His whole body seemed to grow great bubbles, and she jumped back, away from him.

The bubbles popped.

And Carlo was gone. All that remained was a huge, ugly toad.

A cry of fury rent the skies. The dragon roared, and the earth was set afire with a lightning strike of flame.

The dragon rose high, high in the sky, and began a descent, speeding down toward Marina.

Just in time, Michelo made it to stand at her side. He raised his sword. The dragon, so intent on Marina that it was blinded, soared straight into the tip of the blade.

There was another huge and horrible cry.

The dragon fell, causing the earth to tremble.

Radifini came rushing forward, this time talking to Michelo.

"Kiss it!"

"I've kissed it with steel!" Michelo shouted.

"No, kiss it!" Radifini said.

And Marina and Armand and Daphne, and all the guards who had seen what had happened to Carlo, shouted out, "Kiss it!"

Michelo, thinking they had all lost their minds in the frenzy of battle, bent over and kissed the dragon.

Smoke, in a sparking puff of brilliant color, burst from the dragon.

And there . . . soon, as the smoke began to clear . . .

There were two. Two beings.

Two—the dragon, quite unlike a horrible, mean, fire-breathing creature at all.

Indeed, it was actually, quite adorable. Like an overgrown puppy!

But by the dragon's side, having split from its form, there was something else.

No. Someone else. Someone who had taken over the form of the dragon.

For the briefest of moments, they saw the true face of the evil that had threatened them. Not so much in magic now. But in hatred, vengeance, bitterness, and greed.

Moaning, injured, in the midst of the multicolored mist, lay Geovana. Sorceress, witch, the things within her heart having made her the cruelest of enemies. She had walked with a smile so often, while jealousy and a coveting of others had ruled her every action.

And then . . . Geovana began to bubble.

"Back up!" Marina warned.

And they all did.

Bubbles grew and grew . . . and then there was a mighty *pop!*

"Ugh!" said Armand, jumping back quickly to avoid being splashed by the wretched bubble brew.

There, where Geovana had lain, there was nothing but another nasty-looking, injured toad.

It let out a furious croaking.

Then, the toad that had been Carlo croaked, as well.

And both croaking in loud, dissonant tones, as if they argued still, they hopped off together.

The wartrolls melted into the ground.

"The Dragon in the Den! It's really a sweet and gentle creature!" Daphne cried out.

The dragon shyly lowered his head. His ears twitched, he blushed shyly, and he wagged what had once seemed a ferocious tail.

Adriana, Michelo's dear little sister, rushed forward, anxious that no one should now injure the creature. "Please . . . let the dragon go now! We've all seen! The kindest of creatures can be used by others . . . even in innocence. As we were all used!" she cried out. "Yes! We were used, just as the dragon. We let Geovana instill fear into our hearts, and make us behave as we never should have behaved!"

Michelo picked up his little sister and swung her around. "She's right! Everyone must let the dragon live in peace!"

Atop the cliff, people began to cheer.

The beautiful falcon flew over to where Marina stood with her beloved Michelo and friends. Together, they knew the strength of the wartrolls, and even that of the fiercest dragon.

The great Fiorelli, having heard the news of the dungeon breaks and the terrible battle, arrived upon his horse, and with gladness and amazement saw what had been done.

He dismounted from his horse and walked to where his weary son stood with the lady of his heart. He looked from Michelo to Marina and cried out, "A wedding, a wedding tonight! For Christmas nears, and we must make Christmas Day one of joy and thankfulness, and you two duly wed. Man and wife. We will celebrate a time of peace and wonder—and belief. You have proven that there can be no appeasing a dragon, that evil can wear a pleasant mask, and that belief and honor—and the courage to fight for what we love—is the greatest magic! And then we will all remember Christmas is a time for strength in belief, a time of love and goodness."

And so, Michelo kissed his soon-to-be bride. And that time, he kissed her as a lover should, and all around them was applause and the sound of cheering.

When the kiss broke at last—by that time, many of the tired warriors were sitting and wondering if it would be over by sunset—Michelo turned to his father.

"A wedding, Father? There must be two weddings!"

And, of course, the great Duke Fiorelli turned to Armand and Daphne. "Yes, two weddings. And you, falcon master! Armand, you will take the title of the Lord of Baristo, and with Daphne, child of Pietro, and our very good friend, you will live in the castle, and bring peace and prosperity to all the folk there!"

Again, there were cheers.

Armand, not to be outdone, even by Michelo, kissed his soon-to-be bride.

This time, the people cheered, but then groaned as the kiss went on and on, and they were forced to sit and wait once again.

"Good heavens!" Radifini cried. "We will never get to these weddings!"

And so, for the moment, the kissing was over.

Before dressing for her wedding, Marina spoke tenderly and privately with the falcon, Thomasina, thanking her sincerely for all that she had done.

Thomasina reminded Marina that she had never used her final wish.

"Wishes are precious, and must be thought out with grave attention to detail," Marina told her, smiling. "And I have thought . . . and what I wish now is that you are returned to all your strength, that you are able to be all that you want to be, just as you have enabled me!"

"You are sure?" Thomasina asked her.

"Oh, yes. You've taught us all that we must help ourselves, and one another, to make our wishes come true. There is nothing I want more than to share the happiness I feel."

Thomasina raised her wing and gently touched Marina's cheek.

"Leave me be then, child, and get ready for your wedding!"

There had not been such rejoicing in all the territories of Calasia in years. By sunset, before moonrise, Marina was married to Michelo, and Armand became husband to his Daphne.

Champagne flowed. People danced and sang.

And the world itself seemed magic.

Christmas Day came soon after.

When she awoke, after the most magical days ever, Marina raced to the balcony of her new garden room at the castle of the great Fiorelli. (He planned to retire from being duke, leave the realm to his son and Marina, and take his wife on an extended cruise of the known world, until such time as they should return to play with the grandchildren.)

To her astonishment, a falcon perched outside her window.

"Thomasina?" she said, and she was startled, for there was no reply other than a blink of the eyes. Marina realized that, beautiful and wonderful, Thomasina was a falcon. Rare and precious in what she was, but just that, and nothing more. The magic within her was gone.

Michelo came out to the balcony, and he drew her into his arms, startled by the tears in her eyes.

"My love! It is Christmas Day. The church bells are ringing, and we are together. We have our lives to live to bring to others what Christmas magic has brought to us."

"It's just . . . the falcon, Michelo. We must care for her, my falcon, with the greatest tenderness, all of her days!" she told him.

And he, surprised by her strange emotion, but touched by it, held her gently, and said, "We will love her, and care for her always."

Later that day, after the church service, a magical, beautiful snow began to fall. It was the most beautiful snow Marina could remember. And with carols filling the air and more feasting going on—it was really, really, a big celebration—Marina saw that Radifini was not alone. He was with an older woman, beautiful and regal.

They appeared quite happy.

They were giddy, in fact, like children, whispering to one another about magic and belief and all that

kind of thing.

As if aware that Marina was watching her, the woman looked up. She wore a strange, lovely smile of amusement, and Marina was suddenly reminded of the day she had found the falcon, when Carlo had been out hunting, when he had wounded the bird.

At first, she had seen something . . . an animal.

And then a woman . . .

And when she had searched, she had found Thomasina. The gorgeous, magical creature that had claimed to be a fairy.

The woman winked.

And Marina smiled, and turned away. Yet, she paused again. For they were not the only happy couple to be seen together.

Serafina had returned. And she was at the banquet table, seated beside Pietro. Her stepfather was beaming.

Serafina was flushed and exceptionally beautiful, and apparently very pleased to be right where she was.

And Pietro! For once, he seemed truly at ease. Marina realized that she had never really known him before; perhaps he had never really known himself. Now, he was free, as well. And being free . . .

Well, he'd never actually been a *bad* man.

Marina's happiness increased. Sometimes dragons came into the world. But they could be fought, when there was love and courage and conviction. And sometimes, when such demons were bested, there was tremendous beauty to be found.

The woman with Radifini was still watching her.

"Merry Christmas!" the woman called.

"Merry Christmas!" Marina called back happily.

Seeking Michelo, she went off to find—and make—her own magic. Life was the magic one made it, she knew. But Christmas . . .

It would always be a special time of magic. For magic was in belief.

Naturally, in the beautiful fairy-tale realm of Calasia, they all lived happily ever after.

Heather Graham

New York Times and *USA Today* best-selling author Heather Graham majored in theater arts at the University of South Florida. After a stint of several years in dinner theater, back-up vocals, and bartending, she stayed home after the birth of her third child and began to write. Her first book was with Dell, and since then, she has written over one hundred novels and novellas including category, suspense, historical romance, vampire fiction, time travel, occult, and Christmas family fare.

She is pleased to have been published in approximately twenty languages. She has written over 100 novels and has 60 million books in print. She has been honored with awards from Walden Books, B. Dalton, Georgia Romance Writers, Affaire de Coeur, Romantic Times, and more. Heather has also become the proud recipient of the Silver Bullet from Thriller Writers. Heather has had books selected for the Doubleday Book Club and the Literary Guild, and has been quoted, interviewed, or featured in such publications as *The Nation*, *Redbook*, *Mystery Book Club*, *People*, and *USA Today* and appeared on many newscasts including *Today*, *Entertainment Tonight*, and local television.

Heather loves travel and anything that has to do with the water, and is a certified scuba diver. She also loves ballroom dancing. Each year she hosts the Vampire Ball and Dinner theater at the RT convention raising money for the Pediatric Aids Society, and in 2006 she hosted the first Writers for New Orleans Workshop to benefit the stricken Gulf region. She is "thrilled" to be a Thriller Killerette in the Thriller Killer Band, and she is also the founder of "The Slush Pile Players," presenting something that's almost like entertainment for various conferences and benefits. Married since high school graduation and the mother of five, her greatest love in life remains her family, but she also believes her career has been an incredible gift, and she is grateful every day to be doing something that she loves so very much for a living.

The Death Dealer, a hardcover sequel to *The Dead Room*, was released April 2008. The Flynn Brothers Trilogy will be released in late September, *Deadly Gift* in late October, *Deadly Harvest* in early November, and in late November, *Deadly Night*.

www.theoriginalheathergraham.com

Kane Photography ©2008

Cherif Fortin

Lynn Sanders

Cherif Fortin is a freelance photographer, illustrator, and writer living in Chicago, Illinois. At one time he has worked as a professional stuntman, as a full-time firefighter, and as one of the country's leading romance cover models. Cherif's artwork has been featured on the covers of hundreds of books in dozens of countries, and on calendars and collectibles. He runs the successful Fortin & Sanders Studio along with partner, Lynn Sanders, producing commercial art and photography for leading clients internationally. He lives with his wife, Dawn, and their three children: Kira, Kai, and Lara.

Lynn Sanders is an artist, photographer, and writer of romance fiction and children's books. She is co-owner of Fortin & Sanders Studio, which produces cover art for some of the top publishers in the world. Her paintings have been exhibited at Epcot Center and are owned by private collectors such as Hugh Hefner and Fabio. She has three adult children, three grandchildren, and one great-grandchild. She lives in northern Illinois with Ce Ce, her faithful Cirneco dell Etna.

www.fortinandsanders.com

For more information about other
great titles from Medallion Press, visit

medallionpress.com